# Teacher Guide

## LEVEL E

# VOCABULARY

word meaning, pronunciation, prefixes, suffixes, synonyms, antonyms, and fun!

# in Action

LOYOLA PRESS.

Chicago

## LOYOLA PRESS.

3441 N. Ashland Avenue
Chicago, Illinois 60657
(800) 621-1008
www.loyolapress.com

Cover & Interior Art: Anni Betts
Cover Design: Judine O'Shea
Interior Design: Kathy Greenholdt and Joan Bledig

Manufactured in the United States of America.

ISBN-10: 0-8294-2778-3

ISBN-13: 978-0-8294-2778-3

Hess Print Solutions / Woodstock, Illinois USA / 12-09 / 2nd printing

**VISIT**
**www.vocabularyinaction.com**
ACCESS CODE: **VTB-8994**

# Contents

This key shows the meanings of the abbreviations and symbols used throughout the book.

Some English words have more than one possible pronunciation. This book gives only one pronunciation per word, except when different pronunciations indicate different parts of speech. For example, when the word *relay* is used as a noun, it is pronounced rē´ lā; as a verb, the word is pronounced rə lā´.

## Parts of Speech

| | | | | | |
|---|---|---|---|---|---|
| *adj.* | adjective | *int.* | interjection | *prep.* | preposition |
| *adv.* | adverb | *n.* | noun | *part.* | participle |
| | | | | *v.* | verb |

## Vowels

| | | | | | |
|---|---|---|---|---|---|
| ā | tape | ə | about, circus | ôr | torn |
| a | map | ī | kite | oi | noise |
| âr | stare | i | win | ou | foul |
| ä | car, father | ō | toe | o͞o | soon |
| ē | meet | o | mop | o͝o | book |
| e | kept | ô | law | u | tug |

## Consonants

| | | | | | |
|---|---|---|---|---|---|
| ch | check | ŋ | rang | y | yellow |
| g | girl | th | thimble | zh | treasure |
| j | jam | th | that | sh | shelf |

## Stress

The accent mark follows the syllable receiving the major stress, such as in the word *plaster* (plas´ tər).

*Vocabulary in Action* is the premier vocabulary development program that increases students' literacy skills and improves test scores.

Researchers and educators agree that vocabulary development is essential in learning how to communicate effectively through listening, speaking, reading, and writing. The National Reading Panel (2000) has identified vocabulary as one of the five areas that increase students' reading ability. After the third grade, reading difficulties are often attributed to a vocabulary deficit—an inability to understand word meaning.

*Vocabulary in Action* offers the following elements to help students develop this critical literacy skill:

- Flexible leveling and student placement for individualized instruction

- Words that were researched and selected specifically for frequency, occurrence, and relevance to assessment and everyday life

- Intentional, direct instruction focused on words and their meanings, usage, and relationships to other words

- Repeated word appearance in a variety of contexts for extensive exposure and practice with literal and figurative meanings

- Application of new vocabulary skills through practice exercises, assessments, and standardized test preparation opportunities

# Program Overview

## Each Student Book includes

- **Program Pretest** to identify level of understanding

- **Research-based Word Lists** selected for frequency, occurrence, and relevance to assessment

- **One Hundred or More Related Words** including synonyms and antonyms

- **Word Pronunciations, Meanings, and Identifications of Parts of Speech**

- **At Least a Dozen Activities per Chapter,** including activities for words in context, word meaning, word usage, related words, and word building

- **Challenge Words and Activities**

- **Fun with Words** activities for additional practice

- **Test-Taking Tips** section covering test-taking skills, testing formats, and study of testing vocabulary including classic roots, prefixes, and suffixes

- **Special Features** for etymology, mnemonic devices, historical facts, word trivia, and word origin

- **Notable Quotes** that show words in context

- **Chapter Review Assessments** for multiple chapters

- **Program Posttest** to determine overall growth

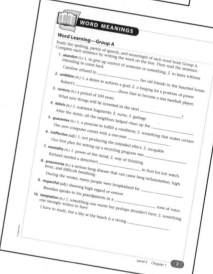

## Total Vocabulary Word Count by Level

| LEVEL | WORDS TO KNOW | ADDITIONAL WORDS |
|-------|---------------|------------------|
| D | 150 | over 100 |
| E | 225 | over 150 |
| F, G, H | 375 | over 200 |

# Each Teacher Guide includes

- **Annotated Guide** similar to the student book for easy correction

- **Additional Games and Activities** for a variety of groupings, learning styles, multiple intelligences, and levels of proficiency in English

- **Suggestions for Guided and Independent Practice**

- **Academic Language Practice** with games and activities, including work with classic roots

- **Icons** for easy identification

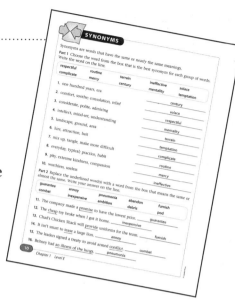

# The *Vocabulary in Action* Web site includes

- Assessments

- Pretests and Reviews

- Word Lists and Definitions

- Vocabulary Games

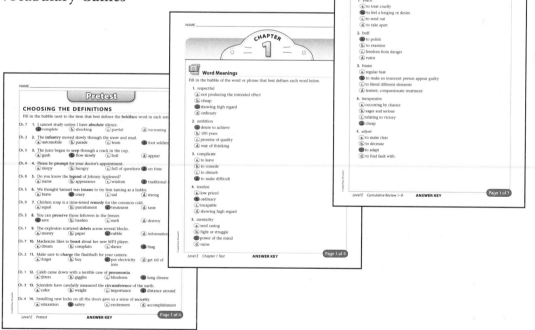

# How to Implement This Program

With *Vocabulary in Action*, it is easy to differentiate instruction to meet the needs of all students.

## Student Placement

Use the following chart to help determine the book most appropriate for each individual student. Differences in level include word difficulty, sentence complexity, and ideas presented in context. In addition to the chart, consider a student's achievement level on any pretest that you give. Adjust books based on a student's achievement on a pretest and other vocabulary assignments, his or her ability to retain new information, and the student's overall work ethic and interest level.

### Placement Levels

| Typical Grade-Level Assignments | | Accelerated Grade-Level Assignments | |
|---|---|---|---|
| LEVEL | GRADE | LEVEL | GRADE |
| D | 4 | D | 3 |
| E | 5 | E | 4 |
| F | 6 | F | 5 |
| G | 7 | G | 6 |
| H | 8 | H | 7 |

## To Begin

At the beginning of the year, choose a book for each student based on the above criteria. Have each student take the program pretest in his or her book. Avoid timing the test. Give students enough time to complete the test thoughtfully and with confidence. After grading the test and noting student achievement levels, make book adjustments if necessary.

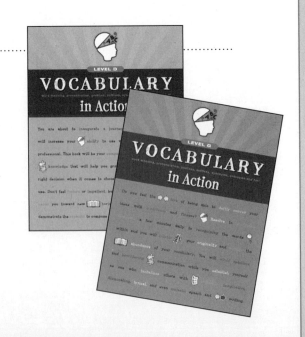

# Work Through the Chapters

Follow these steps to implement each chapter.

1. **Chapter opener:** Have students work with partners, in small groups, or with you to read aloud each word in the **Word List.** Check pronunciation and discuss the definition of each word, having students find the words in a dictionary if you have time. Have students review the **Word Study** section. Introduce the **Challenge Words** in the same way as the Word List. Then have students remove the page and complete the back side.

2. **Chapter pages:** Based on students' confidence and ability, assign students to complete chapter activities independently, with you, with peers, or as homework. Students should complete activities for Words in Context, Word Meanings, Use Your Vocabulary, Word Learning, Synonyms, Antonyms, Word Study, Challenge Words, and Fun with Words. Provide support through modeling and discussion. Here are some approaches:

   - Teacher presents and completes a page with students during the first 10 or 15 minutes of each reading or language arts session. Pages are reviewed simultaneously as guided practice.

   - Students complete chapter pages in class after other reading or language arts assignments are complete. Pages are collected and reviewed after class.

   - Students complete chapter pages as homework assignments, one page per night. Pages are collected and reviewed after completion.

3. **Reteaching/additional practice:** Monitor student progress on a regular basis. If students need additional practice, use the **Games & Activities** on pages 117–122 of this guide or the **Teacher Activities** on pages 123–124.

4. **Standardized test preparation:** At least one month prior to standardized testing, work with students to complete pages 113–114.

5. **Chapter reviews:** After completing every three chapters, administer the Chapter Review to note students' progress and to identify difficult words.

6. **Assessment:** Have students complete a formal assessment after each chapter. Visit **www.vocabularyinaction.com** and access the assessment with this code: **VTB-8994.** You can also access a **Pretest** and **Review.**

# Sample Yearly Plan for Level E

Following is one way to implement *Vocabulary in Action* for Level E.

| WEEK | STUDENT BOOK | RELATED ACTIVITIES |
|---|---|---|
| 1 | Pretest | |
| 2–4 | Chapter 1 | Games & Activities (pp. 117–122)<br>Teacher Activities (pp. 123–124)<br>Chapter 1 Assessment |
| 5–7 | Chapter 2 | Games & Activities (pp. 117–122)<br>Teacher Activities (pp. 123–124)<br>Chapter 2 Assessment |
| 8–11 | Chapter 3 | Games & Activities (pp. 117–122)<br>Teacher Activities (pp. 123–124)<br>Chapter 3 Assessment |
| 12 | Review<br>Chapters 1–3 | Online Games (www.vocabularyinaction.com)<br>Cumulative Review |
| 13–15 | Chapter 4 | Games & Activities (pp. 117–122)<br>Teacher Activities (pp. 123–124)<br>Chapter 4 Assessment |
| 16–18 | Chapter 5 | Games & Activities (pp. 117–122)<br>Teacher Activities (pp. 123–124)<br>Chapter 5 Assessment |
| 19–22 | Chapter 6 | Games & Activities (pp. 117–122)<br>Teacher Activities (pp. 123–124)<br>Chapter 6 Assessment |
| 23 | Review<br>Chapters 4–6 | Online Games (www.vocabularyinaction.com)<br>Cumulative Review |
| 24–26 | Chapter 7 | Games & Activities (pp. 117–122)<br>Teacher Activities (pp. 123–124)<br>Chapter 7 Assessment |
| 27–29 | Chapter 8 | Games & Activities (pp. 117–122)<br>Teacher Activities (pp. 123–124)<br>Chapter 8 Assessment |
| 30–33 | Chapter 9 | Games & Activities (pp. 117–122)<br>Teacher Activities (pp. 123–124)<br>Chapter 9 Assessment |
| 34 | Review<br>Chapters 7–9 | Online Games (www.vocabularyinaction.com)<br>Cumulative Review |
| 35 | Posttest | |

# Pretest

This test contains some of the words you will find in this book. It will give you an idea of the kinds of words you will study. When you have completed all the units, the posttest will measure what you have learned.

## CHOOSING THE DEFINITIONS

Fill in the bubble next to the item that best defines the word in bold in each sentence.

Ch. 7   **1.** The **aggressive** football player ran through the line and scored.
     **a.** tired      **b.** bold      **c.** winning      **d.** lucky

Ch. 1   **2.** After the tornado, the neighborhood was covered with **debris.**
     **a.** sunshine      **b.** leaves      **c.** reporters      **d.** wreckage

Ch. 6   **3.** The workers met with the **administrator** to discuss the new rules.
     **a.** advertiser      **b.** preacher      **c.** lawyer      **d.** director

Ch. 9   **4.** A brown bear **greedily** rummaged through our groceries.
     **a.** quickly      **b.** selfishly      **c.** angrily      **d.** shyly

Ch. 4   **5.** The school band gave an **exceptional** performance at the contest.
     **a.** outstanding      **b.** extra      **c.** terrible      **d.** average

Ch. 8   **6.** Kayla's new ring has a **genuine** diamond.
     **a.** huge      **b.** beautiful      **c.** real      **d.** artificial

Ch. 5   **7.** The farmer owns one thousand **acres.**
     **a.** oak trees      **b.** units of land      **c.** miles      **d.** animals

Ch. 3   **8.** The church choir will hold a bake sale in **conjunction** with the spring concert.
     **a.** association      **b.** opposition      **c.** advance      **d.** evening

Ch. 2   **9.** A deadly **infection** wiped out the state's squirrel population.
     **a.** weapon      **b.** look      **c.** disease      **d.** hunter

Ch. 9   **10.** In science class, Ryan **disassembled** a telephone.
     **a.** experimented      **b.** took apart      **c.** built      **d.** dialed

Ch. 3   **11.** His father's advice had an **influence** on John's decision.
     **a.** power      **b.** explanation      **c.** thought      **d.** memory

Ch. 4   **12.** Conserving energy is good for the earth's **atmosphere.**
     **a.** oceans      **b.** soil      **c.** people      **d.** air

Ch. 7   **13.** The play was an **absolute** success.
     **a.** complete      **b.** former      **c.** unexpected      **d.** fake

**Ch. 2 14.** After his high school graduation, Zachary joined the **infantry.**
   - (a.) babies
   - (b.) party
   - (c.) army
   - (d.) class

**Ch. 6 15.** Abigail was caught in a storm because she failed to **observe** changes in the sky.
   - (a.) ignore
   - (b.) notice
   - (c.) wait for
   - (d.) exit

**Ch. 8 16.** Guards patrolled the **frontier** to keep out illegal visitors.
   - (a.) border
   - (b.) door
   - (c.) jail
   - (d.) mountain

**Ch. 5 17.** My **intention** was to finish all my homework before the big game.
   - (a.) feeling
   - (b.) problem
   - (c.) record
   - (d.) plan

**Ch. 2 18.** My favorite pet is my colorful male **guppy.**
   - (a.) snake
   - (b.) large parrot
   - (c.) small fish
   - (d.) guinea pig

**Ch. 7 19.** Drinking **impure** water can cause serious illness.
   - (a.) warm
   - (b.) dirty
   - (c.) cold
   - (d.) bottled

**Ch. 9 20.** During the long, snowy winter, Brianna **yearned** for the sight of a flower.
   - (a.) wished
   - (b.) detested
   - (c.) searched
   - (d.) yawned

**Ch. 3 21.** The campers found an **adequate** supply of food at the country grocery store.
   - (a.) small
   - (b.) satisfactory
   - (c.) tasty
   - (d.) stale

**Ch. 2 22.** The charity made an **appeal** for donations of canned goods.
   - (a.) request
   - (b.) collection
   - (c.) feast
   - (d.) rejection

**Ch. 8 23.** The approach of the huge elephant **alarmed** some of the children.
   - (a.) annoyed
   - (b.) comforted
   - (c.) growled
   - (d.) scared

**Ch. 3 24.** The designer found a **novel** solution to the problem.
   - (a.) unusual
   - (b.) common
   - (c.) practical
   - (d.) quick

**Ch. 1 25.** We begged Dad to show **mercy** when our pig chewed up his shoe.
   - (a.) training
   - (b.) food
   - (c.) forgiveness
   - (d.) thanks

**Ch. 8 26.** The arrival of a skunk caused a **commotion** among the campers.
   - (a.) boredom
   - (b.) disturbance
   - (c.) peace
   - (d.) teamwork

**Ch. 9 27.** That baseball player is a spokesperson for the sports drink **industry.**
   - (a.) business
   - (b.) warehouse
   - (c.) craze
   - (d.) equipment

**Ch. 3 28.** The program will **conclude** with a speech by the principal.
   - (a.) continue
   - (b.) end
   - (c.) begin
   - (d.) feature

**Ch. 2 29.** David **abused** his good clothes by wearing them to play soccer.
   - (a.) ironed
   - (b.) put on
   - (c.) admired
   - (d.) mistreated

*Pretest   Level E*

NAME _____

**Ch. 8 30.** The artist painted quickly, slapping **vivid** spots of color onto the canvas.
(a.) ugly          (b.) dull          (c.) bright          (d.) round

**Ch. 7 31.** The **incident** at the mall marked the beginning of our friendship.
(a.) sale          (b.) show          (c.) happening          (d.) contest

**Ch. 3 32.** Exercise improves the **circulation** of blood in our bodies.
(a.) color          (b.) flow          (c.) cells          (d.) clotting

**Ch. 9 33.** The players on the opposing teams felt **mutual** respect.
(a.) lack of          (b.) new          (c.) shared          (d.) earned

**Ch. 3 34.** The weather forecaster was **astonished** by the huge snowstorm approaching.
(a.) amazed          (b.) bored          (c.) buried          (d.) chilled

**Ch. 5 35.** Water began to **seep** through the crack in the pipe.
(a.) leak          (b.) pour          (c.) cool          (d.) pull

**Ch. 1 36.** Solving the problem calls for the **mentality** of a scientist.
(a.) books          (b.) computer          (c.) salary          (d.) intellect

**Ch. 5 37.** Olivia's sprained ankle made her an **awkward** dancer.
(a.) graceful          (b.) ballet          (c.) clumsy          (d.) slow

**Ch. 4 38.** With his father by his side, Anthony felt a sense of **security.**
(a.) anger          (b.) safety          (c.) fright          (d.) sadness

**Ch. 8 39.** The ancient **legend** explains why giraffes have long necks.
(a.) tale          (b.) storyteller          (c.) law          (d.) ruin

**Ch. 6 40.** The **course** of the marathon was long and rugged.
(a.) runner          (b.) route          (c.) time          (d.) race

**Ch. 7 41.** The workers teamed up to **reclaim** the old house.
(a.) move into          (b.) buy          (c.) fix up          (d.) destroy

**Ch. 2 42.** The hotel staff did everything they could to **accommodate** the guests.
(a.) scare          (b.) disturb          (c.) feed          (d.) assist

**Ch. 4 43.** Trading in the stock market is one way to **acquire** money.
(a.) lose          (b.) invest          (c.) get          (d.) donate

**Ch. 9 44.** My aunt and I discussed my **compensation** for the babysitting job.
(a.) pay          (b.) rules          (c.) time          (d.) children

**Ch. 5 45.** Taking too many risks is **insane** behavior.
(a.) calm          (b.) pleasant          (c.) usual          (d.) foolish

**Ch. 7 46.** Years ago people read by the light of **kerosene** lamps.
- (a.) dim
- (b.) oil
- (c.) electric
- (d.) bright

**Ch. 1 47.** The student council made a plan to prevent after-school **combat.**
- (a.) fights
- (b.) sports
- (c.) homework
- (d.) activities

**Ch. 1 48.** Unfortunately, the plan was **ineffective.**
- (a.) powerful
- (b.) outdated
- (c.) weak
- (d.) honest

**Ch. 5 49.** Emma's hand felt **numb** after she caught the line drive.
- (a.) warm
- (b.) swollen
- (c.) painful
- (d.) without feeling

**Ch. 6 50.** It can be hard to **adjust** to a new school when you move.
- (a.) get used to
- (b.) be afraid of
- (c.) be taken to
- (d.) get out of

**Ch. 1 51.** Reading is an **inexpensive** way to pass the time.
- (a.) intelligent
- (b.) useful
- (c.) economical
- (d.) exciting

**Ch. 6 52.** Farmers in dry climates need a good **irrigation** system.
- (a.) cleaning
- (b.) watering
- (c.) feeding
- (d.) cooling

**Ch. 2 53.** James made an **earnest** attempt to apologize.
- (a.) careless
- (b.) fake
- (c.) sad
- (d.) sincere

**Ch. 4 54.** Justin went over to get **acquainted** with the new neighbor.
- (a.) forgotten
- (b.) invited
- (c.) introduced
- (d.) ignored

**Ch. 7 55.** "Stop it right now!" Megan growled in a **stern** voice.
- (a.) soft
- (b.) harsh
- (c.) hoarse
- (d.) friendly

**Ch. 4 56.** The hardware store clerk began to **homogenize** the paint.
- (a.) mix
- (b.) pour
- (c.) stack
- (d.) remove

**Ch. 8 57.** Alexander set the clothes he would pack on top of the **bureau.**
- (a.) chest
- (b.) suitcase
- (c.) bed
- (d.) table

**Ch. 6 58.** Grace stayed after school to **oblige** her friend.
- (a.) call
- (b.) meet with
- (c.) ignore
- (d.) help out

**Ch. 9 59.** The tiny amoeba has only one **cell.**
- (a.) eye
- (b.) unit of heat
- (c.) leg
- (d.) living unit of matter

**Ch. 5 60.** Would you **classify** a starfish as a plant or an animal?
- (a.) teach
- (b.) feed
- (c.) sort
- (d.) buy

 **WORD LIST**

Read each word using the pronunciation key.

## Group A

**abandon** (ə ban´ dən)
**ambition** (am bish´ ən)
**century** (sen´ chə rē)
**debris** (də brē´)
**guarantee** (gâr ən tē´)
**ineffective** (in ə fek´ tiv)
**mentality** (men tal´ə tē)
**pneumonia** (noō mōn´ yə)
**respectful** (ri spekt´ fəl)
**temptation** (temp tā´ shən)

## Group B

**annoy** (ə noi´)
**combat** (kom´ bat)
**complicate** (kom´ plə kāt)
**furnish** (fər´ nish)
**inexpensive** (in ik spen´ siv)
**mercy** (mər´ sē)
**pod** (pod)
**routine** (roō tēn´)
**solace** (sol´ is)
**terrain** (tə rān´)

 **WORD STUDY**

## Suffixes

The suffixes -er and -or change an action verb into a noun that names a person who performs the action.

**actor** (ak´ tər) a person who assumes another identity and performs in that role
**counselor** (koun´ səl ər) a person who is trained to give advice
**explorer** (ek splor´ ər) a person who travels to investigate a new place
**inventor** (in vent´ ər) a person who creates something new
**manager** (man´ ə jər) a person who is in charge of a business or a group of people
**writer** (rī´ tər) a person who is the author of stories, poems, or articles

## Challenge Words

**administer** (ad min´ əst ər)
**camouflage** (kam´ ə fläzh)
**centennial** (sen ten´ ē əl)
**combustible** (kəm bəs´ t əb əl)
**dismal** (diz´ məl)

■ **TEACHER TIP:** See page ix for suggestions on how to use this page.

*Level E*

# WORDS IN CONTEXT

Read each sentence below to figure out the meaning of the word in **bold**. Use reasoning skills and the remainder of the sentence to help you. Write the meaning of the word on the line.

1. Jacob tried not to let his pesky little sister's teasing **annoy** him.

   to bother

2. Emily's **ambition** is to become a famous chess grand master.

   goal

3. Every time I turn on the computer to do my homework, I fight the **temptation** to play a game instead.

   urge

4. Exercise should be a part of everyone's daily **routine**.

   habits

5. On our nature walk, we collected dried flowers, leaves, and **pods**.

   natural seed cases, shells, or containers

6. If you follow the trail of **debris**, you'll find a giant monster attacking our city.

   wreckage

7. Some **inexpensive** brands of toothpaste work just as well as the name brands.

   low-priced

8. A **century** from now, will our grandchildren live in a clean environment?

   period of 100 years

9. If you'll **furnish** the cookies, I'll bring the lemonade.

   to supply

10. A shouting match is a really **ineffective** way to solve a problem.

    useless

# WORD MEANINGS

## Word Learning—Group A

Study the spelling, part(s) of speech, and meaning(s) of each word from Group A. Complete each sentence by writing the word on the line. Then read the sentence.

1. **abandon** *(v.)* 1. to give up control of someone or something; 2. to leave without intending to come back

   Caroline refused to _____ abandon _____ her old friends in the haunted house.

2. **ambition** *(n.)* 1. a desire to achieve a goal; 2. a longing for a position of power

   Robert's _____ ambition _____ drove him to become a star baseball player.

3. **century** *(n.)* a period of 100 years

   What new things will be invented in the next _____ century _____?

4. **debris** *(n.)* 1. scattered fragments; 2. ruins; 3. garbage

   After the storm, all the neighbors helped clean up the _____ debris _____.

5. **guarantee** *(n.)* 1. a promise to fulfill a condition; 2. something that makes certain

   The new computer comes with a one-year _____ guarantee _____.

6. **ineffective** *(adj.)* 1. not producing the intended effect; 2. incapable

   Our first plan for setting up a recycling program was _____ ineffective _____.

7. **mentality** *(n.)* 1. power of the mind; 2. way of thinking

   Richard needed a detective's _____ mentality _____ to find his lost watch.

8. **pneumonia** *(n.)* a serious lung disease that can cause lung inflammation, high fever, and difficult breathing

   During the winter, many people were hospitalized for _____ pneumonia _____.

9. **respectful** *(adj.)* showing high regard or esteem

   Brendan speaks to his grandparents in a _____ respectful _____ tone of voice.

10. **temptation** *(n.)* 1. something one wants but perhaps shouldn't have; 2. something one strongly wishes to have

    I have to study, but a day at the beach is a strong _____ temptation _____.

## Use Your Vocabulary—Group A

Choose the word from Group A that best completes each sentence. Write the word on the line. You may use the plural form of nouns and the past tense of verbs if necessary.

More than a(n) __1__ ago, before your grandparents were even born, medicine was not as advanced as it is today. Treatment was often __2__, and many patients did not recover. Common diseases such as __3__, or even a bad case of flu, could cause death. Even though doctors couldn't __4__ that their medicine would work, they never __5__ their patients. Doctors working through the night amid the __6__ of earthquakes and other disasters must have felt a strong __7__ to go away and sleep. But most doctors didn't even think of leaving; it is just not part of their __8__. They stayed as long as they were needed. That dedication is one reason that most people are __9__ toward doctors. Many students today whose __10__ is to have a career in medicine were inspired by stories of those long-ago heroes.

1. _____ century
2. _____ ineffective
3. _____ pneumonia
4. _____ guarantee
5. _____ abandoned
6. _____ debris
7. _____ temptation
8. _____ mentality
9. _____ respectful
10. _____ ambition

## Word Learning—Group B

Study the spelling, part(s) of speech, and meaning(s) of each word from Group B. Complete each sentence by writing the word on the line. Then read the sentence.

1. **annoy** *(v.)* to irritate or disturb

   The dripping sound of that faucet is beginning to _____ annoy _____ me.

2. **combat** *(n.)* 1. a fight with weapons; 2. any fight or struggle

   The soldiers worked hard so they would be prepared for _____ combat _____.

3. **complicate** *(v.)* 1. to make difficult; 2. to confuse

   The extra paperwork will only _____ complicate _____ the process.

4. **furnish** *(v.)* 1. to supply or provide; 2. to provide furniture for a room, house, or office

   The money from your taxes will help _____ furnish _____ the new school.

5. **inexpensive** *(adj.)* cheap, low priced

   That _____ inexpensive _____ coat was made with poor materials.

**6. mercy** *(n.)* 1. showing more kindness than justice requires; 2. lenient, compassionate treatment; 3. something to be thankful for

The judge showed no _____mercy_____ when he sentenced the criminal.

**7. pod** *(n.)* a case, shell, or container in which plants form their seeds

The farmer opened the _____pod_____ and found ripe green peas.

**8. routine** *(n.)* a regular course of procedure; *(adj.)* ordinary

Eating oatmeal is part of our daily morning _____routine_____.

There was nothing _____routine_____ about our trip to Antarctica.

**9. solace** *(v.)* to console; *(n.)* relief of sadness

The coach gave a speech to _____solace_____ her team after the loss.

After arguing with her best friend, Tiffany found _____solace_____ in playing a video game with her brother.

**10. terrain** *(n.)* 1. a piece of land; 2. a geographical area

The campers found it difficult to hike through the rough _____terrain_____.

## Use Your Vocabulary—Group B

Choose the word from Group B that best completes each sentence. Write the word on the line. You may use the plural form of nouns and the past tense of verbs if necessary.

Maybe being a doctor is not your ambition. Have you ever thought about being a park ranger? If you find comfort and **1** in nature, this may be the career for you. Spending time outdoors is part of a ranger's daily **2**. You may find that hikers **3** your job. Many people find hiking through parks a(n) **4** and exciting hobby. It will be your job to **5** aid and information to inexperienced hikers. Hikers may become lost in rugged **6**. They may pick flowers and tramp on rare seed **7**. After all, people and nature are often locked in **8**. But don't let careless hikers **9** you. Have **10** on them. By working with—not against—new hikers, you will teach them to appreciate and protect nature.

1. _____solace_____

2. _____routine_____

3. _____complicate_____

4. _____inexpensive_____

5. _____furnish_____

6. _____terrain_____

7. _____pods_____

8. _____combat_____

9. _____annoy_____

10. _____mercy_____

# SYNONYMS

Synonyms are words that have the same or nearly the same meanings.

**Part 1** Choose the word from the box that is the best synonym for each group of words. Write the word on the line.

| respectful | routine | terrain | ineffective | solace |
|---|---|---|---|---|
| complicate | mercy | century | mentality | temptation |

1. one hundred years, era _____ century

2. comfort, soothe; consolation, relief _____ solace

3. considerate, polite, admiring _____ respectful

4. intellect, mind-set, understanding _____ mentality

5. landscape, ground, area _____ terrain

6. lure, attraction, bait _____ temptation

7. mix up, tangle, make more difficult _____ complicate

8. everyday, typical; practice, habit _____ routine

9. pity, extreme kindness, compassion _____ mercy

10. worthless, useless _____ ineffective

**Part 2** Replace the underlined word(s) with a word from the box that means the same or almost the same. Write your answer on the line.

| guarantee | annoy | pneumonia | abandon | furnish |
|---|---|---|---|---|
| combat | inexpensive | ambition | debris | pod |

11. The company made a <u>promise</u> to have the lowest price. _____ guarantee

12. The <u>cheap</u> toy broke when I got it home. _____ inexpensive

13. Chad's Chicken Shack will <u>provide</u> uniforms for the team. _____ furnish

14. It isn't smart to <u>tease</u> a large lion. _____ annoy

15. The leaders signed a treaty to avoid armed <u>conflict</u>. _____ combat

16. Britney had an <u>illness of the lungs</u>. _____ pneumonia

**17.** The careless campers left <u>trash</u> all over the campsite. _____debris_____

**18.** The twins are as alike as two peas in a <u>shell</u>. _____pod_____

**19.** The climbers had to <u>leave</u> their heavy backpacks. _____abandon_____

**20.** Nicolas's <u>goal</u> is to become a teacher. _____ambition_____

 **ANTONYMS**

Antonyms are words that have opposite or nearly opposite meanings.

**Part 1** Choose the word from the box that is the best antonym for each group of words. Write the word on the line.

| solace | ambition | furnish |
|---|---|---|
| combat | inexpensive | |

**1.** precious, extravagant, costly _____inexpensive_____

**2.** laziness, indifference, lack of purpose _____ambition_____

**3.** peace, agreement _____combat_____

**4.** to take away, remove _____furnish_____

**5.** grief, sadness _____solace_____

**Part 2** Replace the underlined word(s) with a word from the box that means the opposite or almost the opposite. Write your answer on the line.

| mercy | routine | ineffective |
|---|---|---|
| complicate | respectful | |

**6.** Adopting a stray kitten is an act of <u>cruelty</u>. _____mercy_____

**7.** The speaker gave <u>rude</u> answers to the students' questions. _____respectful_____

**8.** The toddler's help was <u>useful</u>. _____ineffective_____

**9.** The sound of a siren is <u>extraordinary</u> in the city. _____routine_____

**10.** The extra chores will <u>simplify</u> our life. _____complicate_____

**Suffixes** Add the suffix *-er* or *-or* to each word. Then write one sentence using the verb form of the word and another sentence using the noun form.

**1.** write + er _____writer_____

Sentence should include the word *write.*

_____

Sentence should include the word *writer.*

_____

**2.** act + or _____actor_____

Sentence should include the word *act.*

_____

Sentence should include the word *actor.*

_____

**3.** explore + er _____explorer_____

Sentence should include the word *explore.*

_____

Sentence should include the word *explorer.*

_____

**4.** invent + or _____inventor_____

Sentence should include the word *invent.*

_____

Sentence should include the word *inventor.*

_____

**5.** manage + er _____manager_____

Sentence should include the word *manage.*

_____

Sentence should include the word *manager.*

_____

**6.** counsel + or _____counselor_____

Sentence should include the word *counsel.*

_____

Sentence should include the word *counselor.*

_____

# CHALLENGE WORDS

## Word Learning—Challenge!

Study the spelling, part(s) of speech, and meaning(s) of each word. Complete each sentence by writing the word on the line. Then read the sentence.

1. **administer** *(v.)* 1. to give out; 2. to manage the use of

   The doctors agreed to _____administer_____ the flu vaccine for free.

2. **camouflage** *(n.)* a disguise of paint, nets, or foliage that makes something look like its surroundings; *(v.)* to give a false appearance

   The soldiers wore _____camouflage_____ to hide in the woods.

   To _____camouflage_____ her gift, Lucy carried it in a brown paper bag.

3. **centennial** *(adj.)* pertaining to a 100th anniversary; *(n.)* the 100th anniversary

   The mayor planned a _____centennial_____ celebration for our town.

   The date of the _____centennial_____ was August 12, 2009.

4. **combustible** *(adj.)* capable of catching fire and burning easily

   Keep all _____combustible_____ materials away from the bonfire.

5. **dismal** *(adj.)* 1. disastrous, dreadful; 2. gloomy

   We postponed our picnic because of the _____dismal_____ weather.

## Use Your Vocabulary—Challenge!

*Party in the Park* The park service is throwing a party, and you're in charge. The celebration will honor Dr. Will Curem, the town's first doctor and the person who donated the parkland to the city. It will be held on the 100th anniversary of Dr. Curem's birth. On a separate sheet of paper, write an announcement about the party for your local newspaper. Tell when, where, and why the party will be held. Make the party sound like fun so that many citizens will come. Use the Challenge Words above.

> ### Vocabulary in Action
>
> The word **dismal** can be traced all the way back to medieval calendars. On those calendars, there were two bad or unlucky days marked for every month. The Latin root *mal* appears in many words that are related to "bad" things, such as *malady* ("sickness"), *malice* ("the desire to do bad things to others"), and *malodor* ("bad smell").

# FUN WITH WORDS

Write the vocabulary word that matches each clue. Put one letter in each blank. Then use the numbered letters to fill in the blanks and solve the riddle.

1. You might cover a lot of this on a hike.  T E R R A I N
   <br>     1

2. This makes a promise.  G U A R A N T E E
   <br>          2   3

3. If you're bored, it might be time to change this.  R O U T I N E
   <br>     4     5  6

4. If you bring a new chair for the room, you're not furniture. But you do this.

   F U R N I S H
   <br>7        8

5. What's inside this can keep growing.  P O D
   <br>     9

6. Want to run for president? You'll need lots of this.

   A M B I T I O N
   <br>  10     11

7. If something's on sale, it's probably this.

   I N E X P E N S I V E
   <br>    12

8. Most people don't see a whole one.  C E N T U R Y
   <br>       13    14

9. What's left after a big windstorm.  D E B R I S
   <br>     15     16

10. If something doesn't work the way it's supposed to, it's this.

    I N E F F E C T I V E
    <br>17 18   19   20   21

**Riddle: How can you tell an elephant's been in your refrigerator?**

F O O T P R I N T S   I N
<br>19 11 9 1 12 4 17 2 5 16   6 18

T H E   B U T T E R !
<br>20 8 15   10 7 13 3 21 14

## WORD LIST

Read each word using the pronunciation key.

## Group A

**abuse** (*v.* ə byo͞oz´) (*n.* ə byo͞os´)
**appeal** (ə pēl´)
**channel** (chan´ əl)
**compliment** (kom´ plə mənt)
**distract** (dis trakt´)
**guppy** (gəp´ ē)
**infantry** (in´ fən trē)
**migration** (mī grā´ shən)
**salvation** (sal vā´ shən)
**testimony** (tes´ tə mō nē)

## Group B

**accommodate** (ə kom´ ə dāt)
**charge** (chärj)
**compassion** (kəm pa´ shən)
**earnest** (ər´ nəst)
**infection** (in fek´ shən)
**inherent** (in hir´ ənt)
**molecule** (mo´ li kyo͞ol)
**perilous** (per´ ə ləs)
**sanity** (sa´ nə tē)
**theory** (thē´ ə rē)

## WORD STUDY

### Homophones

Homophones sound the same, but their spellings and definitions are different.

**ascent** (ə sent´) a rising or upward movement
**assent** (ə sent´) an agreement

**capital** (kap´ ə təl) a large letter; the city that is the seat of government
**capitol** (kap´ ə təl) the building that houses a state legislature

**hangar** (haŋ´ ər) a building that houses airplanes
**hanger** (haŋ´ ər) a piece of shaped metal, wood, or plastic used for holding clothing

### Challenge Words
**endurance** (en dur´ əns)
**envious** (en´ vē əs)
**furrow** (fər ō)
**mingle** (miŋ´ gəl)
**modesty** (mod´ ə stē)

■ **TEACHER TIP: See page ix for suggestions on how to use this page.**

## WORDS IN CONTEXT

Read each sentence below to figure out the meaning of the word in **bold.** Use reasoning skills and the remainder of the sentence to help you. Write the meaning of the word on the line.

1. Do you have an **earnest** desire to work with animals?

   _____ sincere _____

2. A career as a veterinarian can **accommodate** your desire.

   _____ to oblige _____

3. If you decide to be a vet, don't let anything **distract** you.

   _____ to lead astray _____

4. Sometimes being a veterinarian can be **perilous.**

   _____ dangerous _____

5. An animal that is usually friendly may **charge** when it is in pain.

   _____ to attack _____

6. Stories of animal **abuse** may upset you.

   _____ mistreatment _____

7. Some animals will seem to **appeal** to you for help.

   _____ to request _____

8. But they'll feel fine when you cure their **infection.**

   _____ disease _____

9. You'll receive **compliments** from happy pet owners.

   _____ praise _____

10. A dog's wagging tail will be **testimony** that you've chosen the right job.

   _____ declaration _____

# WORD MEANINGS

## Word Learning—Group A

Study the spelling, part(s) of speech, and meaning(s) of each word. Complete each sentence by writing the word on the line. Then read the sentence.

1. **abuse** *(v.)* 1. to use improperly; 2. to treat cruelly or roughly; *(n.)* 1. cruel or rough treatment; 2. a deceitful act

   If you _____abuse_____ the privilege, it will be taken away.

   Animal control officers work hard to prevent animal _____abuse_____.

2. **appeal** *(n.)* an earnest request for help or sympathy; *(v.)* 1. to ask for help; 2. to ask that a case be taken to a higher court in the judicial system

   The director of the food bank made an _____appeal_____ for donations.

   The lawyer promised to _____appeal_____ the case to the Supreme Court.

3. **channel** *(n.)* the deeper part of a river or stream; *(v.)* to make a groove

   The ship may run aground if it does not follow the _____channel_____.

   Laborers worked for years to _____channel_____ a canal to connect the two oceans.

4. **compliment** *(n.)* an admiring remark said about a person or thing

   The teacher's _____compliment_____ made Hannah blush.

5. **distract** *(v.)* to draw away one's attention to a different object or in many directions at once

   The sound of a TV may _____distract_____ you from your reading.

6. **guppy** *(n.)* a tiny fish of tropical fresh water, sometimes kept in aquariums

   If you don't have much room for a pet, try keeping a _____guppy_____.

7. **infantry** *(n.)* soldiers trained, organized, and equipped to fight on foot

   Dad was awarded a medal for serving in the _____infantry_____.

8. **migration** *(n.)* moving from one place to another

   Flocks of geese fly in the shape of a wedge during their yearly _____migration_____.

9. **salvation** *(n.)* 1. a saving; 2. preservation from destruction or failure

   The _____salvation_____ of swimmers in peril is a lifeguard's most important job.

**10. testimony** *(n.)* 1. a solemn statement used for evidence or proof; 2. a solemn declaration

Avery was happy to offer _____testimony_____ that showed his friend could not have committed the crime.

## Use Your Vocabulary—Group A

Choose the word from Group A that best completes each sentence. Write the word on the line. You may use the plural form of nouns and the past tense of verbs if necessary.

Michael Gomez always thought he would serve in the **1** when he grew up. Then he heard a(n) **2** from a speaker for the National Park Service who was asking for help. "Our parks are in great need of **3** ," the speaker said. "If you care about nature and enjoy working outdoors, don't let anything **4** you from becoming a forest ranger." From that time on, Michael volunteered his time to protect the environment from **5** . At a city council meeting, Michael gave **6** about saving the city park. He presented a plan to **7** a canal from the pond to water plants. He made a list of flowers that attract monarch butterflies during their yearly **8** to Mexico. He offered to organize a sale of goldfish and **9** to raise money for park improvements. Michael received many **10** for his conservation work. But the most important thing, Michael knows, is that he is getting experience that will help him in his future career.

1. _____infantry_____

2. _____appeal_____

3. _____salvation_____

4. _____distract_____

5. _____abuse_____

6. _____testimony_____

7. _____channel_____

8. _____migration_____

9. _____guppies_____

10. _____compliments_____

### Vocabulary in Action

"Our inventions are wont to be pretty toys, which **distract** our attention from serious things. They are but improved means to an unimproved end."

—Henry David Thoreau (1817–1862), author, naturalist (from *Walden*)

# Word Learning—Group B

Study the spelling, part(s) of speech, and meaning(s) of each word from Group B. Complete each sentence by writing the word on the line. Then read the sentence.

1. **accommodate** *(v.)* 1. to help out; 2. to give something wanted or needed

   The baseball player seemed happy to _____accommodate_____ our desire for an autograph.

2. **charge** *(v.)* 1. to put electricity into; 2. to attack; *(n.)* 1. a price; 2. an accusation

   The computer won't work until you _____charge_____ the battery.

   The defendant swore she was not guilty of the _____charge_____ of theft.

3. **compassion** *(n.)* pity; sympathy

   The police officer showed _____compassion_____ for the injured criminal.

4. **earnest** *(adj.)* 1. strong and intense in purpose; 2. eager and serious

   Even though they were playing against the league champions, our team made an _____earnest_____ effort to win.

5. **infection** *(n.)* disease in humans and animals caused by contact with germs

   Washing your hands often will help you avoid _____infection_____.

6. **inherent** *(adj.)* 1. involving a necessary characteristic of something; 2. belonging by nature

   Koalas have an _____inherent_____ need for eucalyptus leaves.

7. **molecule** *(n.)* the smallest particle of a substance that retains the chemical identity of the substance

   All matter is made up of tiny _____molecules_____.

8. **perilous** *(adj.)* dangerous

   The rescue effort included a _____perilous_____ trip across rugged mountains.

9. **sanity** *(n.)* soundness of mind or mental health

   The lawyer hoped to win the case by asking the jurors to question the _____sanity_____ of the star witness.

10. **theory** *(n.)* 1. an explanation based on observation and reasoning; 2. an opinion or idea

    Every invention begins with a scientific _____theory_____.

## Use Your Vocabulary—Group B

Choose the word from Group B that best completes each sentence. Write the word on the line. You may use the plural form of nouns and the past tense of verbs if necessary.

When she was a child, Kaitlyn Smith suffered from a serious lung __1__. Her kindly doctor treated her with humor and __2__. After she was cured, young Kaitlyn made a(n) __3__ promise to herself to become a doctor. In science class, she studied everything from plants and animals to atoms and __4__. Medical school seemed so hard and long that she wondered how she would keep from losing her __5__. But Dr. Smith's desire to help people was __6__ in her character. After many years of studying, she returned to her old neighborhood to set up her practice. Now Dr. Smith does everything she can to __7__ her patients' needs. If her patients cannot pay, she does not __8__ them. She teaches on the latest __9__ about preventing disease. Even though a doctor's job is sometimes __10__, Kaitlyn Smith would rather be a doctor than anything else.

1. _____ infection
2. _____ compassion
3. _____ earnest
4. _____ molecules
5. _____ sanity
6. _____ inherent
7. _____ accommodate
8. _____ charge
9. _____ theories
10. _____ perilous

# SYNONYMS

Synonyms are words that have the same or nearly the same meanings.

**Part 1** Choose the word from the box that is the best synonym for each group of words. Write the word on the line.

| | | | | |
|---|---|---|---|---|
| distract | accommodate | salvation | abuse | migration |
| compliment | sanity | molecule | compassion | channel |

1. deliverance, rescue, reprieve          _____ salvation

2. depths; carve          _____ channel

3. divert, confuse, lead astray          _____ distract

4. good mental health, sense          _____ sanity

**5.** hurt, mistreat; injury, misuse _____ abuse _____

**6.** praise, tribute _____ compliment _____

**7.** kindness, mercy, respect _____ compassion _____

**8.** movement, journey, travel _____ migration _____

**9.** oblige, assist, help _____ accommodate _____

**10.** unit, particle, bit _____ molecule _____

**Part 2** Replace the underlined word(s) with a word from the box that means the same or almost the same. Write your answer on the line.

| inherent | appeal | perilous | charge | theory |
|----------|--------|----------|--------|--------|
| testimony | infantry | infection | earnest | guppy |

**11.** There will be a small <u>fee</u> for the service. _____ charge _____

**12.** Every year charities <u>ask</u> for financial assistance. _____ appeal _____

**13.** Honesty must be an <u>essential</u> part of a police officer's character. _____ inherent _____

**14.** Skydiving is an exciting but <u>risky</u> hobby. _____ perilous _____

**15.** The doctor said the <u>disease</u> was caused by a virus. _____ infection _____

**16.** The scientists devised an experiment to confirm their <u>idea</u>. _____ theory _____

**17.** After graduation, Faith plans to enlist in the <u>army</u>. _____ infantry _____

**18.** Erica made a <u>solemn</u> promise to do her best work. _____ earnest _____

**19.** Nathan moved his <u>tropical fish</u> to a new aquarium. _____ guppy _____

**20.** The witness's <u>statement</u> helped convict the shoplifter. _____ testimony _____

*Level E   Chapter 2*

 **ANTONYMS**

Antonyms are words that have opposite or nearly opposite meanings.

**Part 1** Choose the word from the box that is the best antonym for each group of words. Write the word on the line.

| channel | salvation | distract |
|---------|-----------|----------|
| earnest | perilous | theory |

1. careless, insincere, not serious      _____ earnest _____

2. focus, concentrate, emphasize      _____ distract _____

3. safe, easy, secure      _____ perilous _____

4. shallows, shore; fill in      _____ channel _____

5. destruction, failure to save      _____ salvation _____

6. fact, certainty, truth      _____ theory _____

**Part 2** Replace the underlined word(s) with a word from the box that means the opposite or almost the opposite. Write your answer on the line.

| accommodate | compliment | sanity | charge |
|-------------|------------|--------|--------|
| compassion | abuse | migration | |

7. Carlos listened to his music teacher's rude comment. _____ compliment _____

8. I know Angelica would never nurture a pig. _____ abuse _____

9. In autumn, many birds begin their yearly staying in one place.
_____ migration _____

10. Xavier showed unkindness by talking to the crying man. _____ compassion _____

11. I knew that the growling cougar would retreat if I kept running.
_____ charge _____

12. The noise in the lunchroom could make you lose your poor mental health.
_____ sanity _____

13. The servers do whatever they can to deny guests.
_____ accommodate _____

# WORD STUDY

**Homophones** Proofread the story. Circle each word that is used incorrectly. Then rewrite the incorrect sentences on the lines below using the correct words.

Our class begged the principal to allow us to take a class trip. The principal gave her (ascent)—but only if we raised the money ourselves. We held many fundraisers. Our best one was a craft sale. We sold useful things such as (hangars) covered with ribbons. We washed cars. We even washed small airplanes in their (hangers) at the local airport. At last we had enough money to fly to our nation's (capitol.) As our plane made its (assent,) we all cheered. We couldn't wait to visit the White House and the (Capital) Building.

1. The principal gave her assent—but only if we raised the money ourselves.

2. We sold useful things such as hangers covered with ribbons.

3. We even washed small airplanes in their hangars at the local airport.

4. At last we had enough money to fly to our nation's capital.

5. As our plane made its ascent, we all cheered.

6. We couldn't wait to visit the White House and the Capitol Building.

# CHALLENGE WORDS

## Word Learning—Challenge!

Study the spelling, part(s) of speech, and meaning(s) of each word. Complete each sentence by writing the word on the line. Then read the sentence.

1. **endurance** *(n.)* the ability to withstand hardship

   Marathon runners need both strength and _____endurance_____.

2. **envious** *(adj.)* feeling dissatisfaction because of wanting what another has

   Alejandra tried not to be _____envious_____ of her sister's musical talent.

3. **furrow** *(n.)* long, narrow groove, as cut in the earth by a plow; *(v.)* to wrinkle

   The farmer began preparing the field by making a _____furrow_____.

   Every time the twins concentrate, they both _____furrow_____ their brows in the same way.

**4. mingle** *(v.)* 1. to bring or mix together; 2. to associate

Serena breathed a sigh of relief as her party guests began to relax and
_____mingle_____.

**5. modesty** *(n.)* 1. not thinking highly of oneself or one's abilities; 2. being shy

Gregory's _____modesty_____ kept him from bragging about winning the
science fair.

## Use Your Vocabulary—Challenge!

*I Have a Dream* Michael Gomez and Kaitlyn Smith each had a dream. They planned
ahead to achieve their goals. What career sounds interesting to you? What will it take
to fulfill your dream? On a separate sheet of paper, write about things you can do now
that will help you achieve your goal. Use the Challenge Words below.

> endurance     envious     furrow     mingle     modesty

## FUN WITH WORDS

Use a vocabulary word to complete each sentence. The word you choose should rhyme
with the word in *italics*.

1. Perhaps you'll accuse me of *vanity*, but I never question my _____sanity_____.

2. I'd rather have a *puppy*, but I'll settle for a(n) _____guppy_____.

3. I don't have powers of *detection*, but this fever says I have a(n) _____infection_____.

4. My bank account isn't *large*, so I can't afford that _____charge_____.

5. This summer's *vacation* will be my _____salvation_____.

Now you try it. On a separate sheet of paper, write rhyming sentences using three of
the following vocabulary words.

> appeal     theory     distract     channel     abuse

# CHAPTER 3

## WORD LIST

Read each word using the pronunciation key.

### Group A

abolish (ə bol´ ish)
accumulate (ə kyōō´ myə lāt)
circulation (sər kyə lā´ shən)
conclude (kən klōōd´)
harmonize (här´ mə nīz)
inflammable (in flam´ ə bəl)
nourish (nər´ ish)
prediction (pri dik´ shən)
satellite (sat´ ə līt)
traitor (trā´ tər)

### Group B

adequate (ad´ i kwət)
astonish (ə ston´ ish)
circumference (sər kum´ frəns)
conjunction (kən junk´ shən)
hoarse (hôrs)
influence (in´ flōō əns)
novel (nov´ əl)
preserve (pri zərv´)
scandal (skan´ dəl)
treaty (trē´ tē)

## WORD STUDY

### Prefixes

The prefix *tele-* means "far away."

**telecommunicate** (tel´ ə kə myōō nə kāt) to send electronic messages over distances

**telephone** (tel´ ə fōn) a machine for sending and receiving speech sounds over distances

**telephoto** (tel´ ə fō tō) a camera lens that makes distant objects appear to be closer

**telescope** (tel´ ə skōp) an instrument that makes distant objects appear to be closer

**television** (tel´ ə vizh ən) a receiver for sound and pictures that are sent over the airwaves

### Challenge Words

**antiquated** (ant´ ə kwāt əd)
**compile** (kəm pīl´)
**deficient** (di fish´ ənt)
**dependent** (di pen´ dənt)
**saturate** (sach´ ə rāt)

■ **TEACHER TIP:** See page ix for suggestions on how to use this page.

*Level E*

# WORDS IN CONTEXT

Read each sentence below to figure out the meaning of the word in **bold**. Use reasoning skills and the remainder of the sentence to help you. Write the meaning of the word on the line.

1. Every subject in school helps you **accumulate** knowledge.

   to gather in
   _____

2. Our teacher assigns us biographies to read, but I would much rather read **novels**.

   fictional book
   _____

3. If **satellites** fascinate you, you will probably find astronomy most interesting.

   moons
   _____

4. In science, you may study the body's blood **circulation** system.

   flow
   _____

5. Even if you're not a great cook, you can learn to make an **adequate** meal in the new cooking class.

   satisfactory
   _____

6. You may learn things in your social studies class that will **astonish** you.

   to amaze
   _____

7. History is filled with exciting adventures and mysterious **scandals**.

   dishonorable acts
   _____

8. One of the most famous historical facts involved the duel of the well-known **traitor** Benedict Arnold.

   betrayer
   _____

9. Have you learned to measure the **circumference** of a circle in math class yet?

   distance around
   _____

10. Students may joke that someone should **abolish** school, but without school, where would you learn so many interesting things?

   to do away with
   _____

# WORD MEANINGS

## Word Learning—Group A

Study the spelling, part(s) of speech, and meaning(s) of each word from Group A. Complete each sentence by writing the word on the line. Then read the sentence.

1. **abolish** *(v.)* to do away with or put an end to

   I hope our school board does not _____abolish_____ the drama program.

2. **accumulate** *(v.)* to pile up or collect

   It takes a long time and hard work to _____accumulate_____ a fortune.

3. **circulation** *(n.)* going around or sending around

   Veins and arteries are part of our body's _____circulation_____ system.

4. **conclude** *(v.)* 1. to end; 2. to make decisions or opinions by reasoning

   The meeting will _____conclude_____ after the president's speech.

5. **harmonize** *(v.)* 1. to add tones to a melody to create chords; 2. to play or sing to a tuneful sound

   The barbershop quartet gets together to _____harmonize_____ weekly.

6. **inflammable** *(adj.)* 1. easily set on fire; 2. easily excited or angered

   Never light a match near an _____inflammable_____ fluid, such as gasoline.

7. **nourish** *(v.)* 1. to help grow, or keep alive and well, with food; 2. to maintain

   This plant food is just what we need to _____nourish_____ the seedlings.

8. **prediction** *(n.)* something told beforehand

   The coach made a _____prediction_____ that our team would win.

9. **satellite** *(n.)* 1. a celestial body that revolves around a planet; 2. a moon; 3. a manufactured object intended to circle a planet

   Soon NASA will launch a new communications _____satellite_____.

10. **traitor** *(n.)* 1. a person who betrays a trust, a duty, or a friend; 2. one who commits treason

    The counterspy admitted that he was a _____traitor_____ to his country.

## Use Your Vocabulary—Group A

Choose the word from Group A that best completes each sentence. Write the word on the line. You may use the plural form of nouns and the past tense of verbs if necessary.

The moon is a(n) __1__ of our planet. For centuries, people made __2__ about what we would find on the moon. Some people __3__ that it was made of green cheese. Finally, the Apollo astronauts were sent to find out what was there. With a fiery burst of __4__ fuel, the rocket was launched. The crew's mission was to __5__ myths about the moon. They __6__ samples of soil and moon rocks. They planned to find out if the moon could support and __7__ any form of life. The astronauts had fun too. Some mornings the ground crew would __8__ in a cheerful wake-up tune. Because the moon has less gravity, the astronauts could jump and play. The lack of air in __9__ on the moon means the footprints they made will never blow away. Only a(n) __10__ would refuse to be proud of our brave astronauts.

1. _____satellite_____

2. _____predictions_____

3. _____concluded_____

4. _____inflammable_____

5. _____abolish_____

6. _____accumulated_____

7. _____nourish_____

8. _____harmonize_____

9. _____circulation_____

10. _____traitor_____

## Word Learning—Group B

Study the spelling, part(s) of speech, and meaning(s) of each word from Group B. Complete each sentence by writing the word on the line. Then read the sentence.

1. **adequate** (*adj.*) enough; sufficient

   Did we pack an ___adequate___ supply of food for the trip?

2. **astonish** (*v.*) to surprise greatly, amaze

   The magician's trick will ___astonish___ the audience.

3. **circumference** (*n.*) the distance around a circle or sphere

   The earth's ___circumference___ is about 25,000 miles.

4. **conjunction** (*n.*) 1. a joining of something with another; 2. union; 3. combination

   The final plan was a ___conjunction___ of both ideas.

5. **hoarse** (*adj.*) 1. rough and deep sounding; 2. having a harsh voice

   After the big game, our voices were ___hoarse___ from cheering.

**6. influence** (*n.*) the act or power of producing an effect without great force

Mom hopes the babysitter will be a good _____influence_____ on us.

**7. novel** (*adj.*) of a new kind; (*n.*) often long, usually complex fictional story

Madison thought of a _____novel_____ solution for the problem.

Would you rather read a _____novel_____ or a history?

**8. preserve** (*v.*) 1. to keep safe from harm or change; 2. to protect or maintain

Mom planned to _____preserve_____ my picture by framing it.

**9. scandal** (*n.*) 1. conduct that brings disgrace or shocks the public; 2. the loss of or damage to reputation

The newspaper reported the shocking _____scandal_____.

**10. treaty** (*n.*) 1. a written, formal agreement between countries; 2. the document that contains the agreement

The heads of state held a meeting to sign the peace _____treaty_____.

## Use Your Vocabulary—Group B

Choose the word from Group B that best completes each sentence. Write the word on the line. You may use the plural form of nouns and the past tense of verbs if necessary.

It seems that there is __1__ room in outer space for everyone. After all, many natural and human-made objects travel around the earth's __2__ without getting in one another's way. But maybe now is the time to draw up a(n) __3__ among the nations to make rules to __4__ outer space as we know it. Already people have had some __5__ ideas for using outer space. Advertisers have suggested working in __6__ with the government to launch a giant lighted billboard into the sky. Are you shocked? Does that idea __7__ you? They think this advertising would have a great __8__ on consumers. Most people I know would shout themselves __9__ fighting that plan. Imagine gazing up at the stars on a warm summer night and seeing a commercial instead! I think advertising in space would be a(n) __10__. Don't you?

1. _____adequate_____

2. _____circumference_____

3. _____treaty_____

4. _____preserve_____

5. _____novel_____

6. _____conjunction_____

7. _____astonish_____

8. _____influence_____

9. _____hoarse_____

10. _____scandal_____

# SYNONYMS

Synonyms are words that have the same or nearly the same meanings.

**Part 1** Choose the word from the box that is the best synonym for each group of words. Write the word on the line.

| | | | | |
|---|---|---|---|---|
| inflammable | harmonize | accumulate | influence | satellite |
| conjunction | circumference | circulation | nourish | conclude |

1. association, joining _____conjunction_____

2. authority, control, power _____influence_____

3. end, finish; decide _____conclude_____

4. distribution, rotation, flow _____circulation_____

5. combustible, explosive, excitable _____inflammable_____

6. moon, space station _____satellite_____

7. perimeter, distance around _____circumference_____

8. gather, store, amass _____accumulate_____

9. sustain, feed, support _____nourish_____

10. be tuneful or melodious _____harmonize_____

**Part 2** Replace the underlined word(s) with a word from the box that means the same or almost the same. Write your answer on the line.

| | | | | |
|---|---|---|---|---|
| scandal | preserve | novel | hoarse | treaty |
| abolish | traitor | adequate | astonish | prediction |

11. The secret I am about to tell you will <u>amaze</u> you. _____astonish_____

12. The <u>pact</u> was signed, and the countries declared peace. _____treaty_____

13. The student who stole our unicorn mascot is a <u>betrayer</u>! _____traitor_____

14. The mayor's bad behavior is a <u>disgrace</u> to our town. _____scandal_____

15. People of all races worked to <u>put an end to</u> slavery. _____abolish_____

**16.** Cameron thinks his grades are <u>satisfactory</u>. _____adequate_____

**17.** The weather reporter's <u>forecast</u> turned out to be wrong. _____prediction_____

**18.** Nicole woke up with a cold and a <u>ragged</u> voice. _____hoarse_____

**19.** The citizens planned a drive to <u>keep</u> the historic building. _____preserve_____

**20.** Writing a <u>long, fictional story</u> is a hard job. _____novel_____

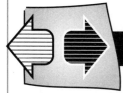 # ANTONYMS

Antonyms are words that have opposite or nearly opposite meanings.

**Part 1** Choose the word from the box that is the best antonym for each group of words. Write the word on the line.

| | | |
|---|---|---|
| **accumulate** | **scandal** | **hoarse** |
| **conjunction** | **novel** | **traitor** |

**1.** distribute, scatter, give away _____accumulate_____

**2.** patriot, loyalist, nationalist _____traitor_____

**3.** typical, usual, familiar _____novel_____

**4.** splitting apart, separation _____conjunction_____

**5.** smooth sounding, soft _____hoarse_____

**6.** good behavior, propriety _____scandal_____

*Vocabulary in Action*

The word *invisible* means "not visible." The word *ineffective* means "not effective." They both use the prefix *in-* to mean "not." But just as words can have more than one meaning, some prefixes have more than one meaning. The prefix *in-* can also mean "inside." For example, *inscribe* means "to write inside something," and *inherent* describes a quality inside something. The word **inflammable** uses the prefix *in-* to mean "inside." Sometimes people think *inflammable* means "not able to be set on fire." In fact, *inflammable* and *flammable* mean the same thing!

**Part 2** Replace the underlined word with a word from the box that means the opposite or almost the opposite. Write your answer on the line.

| | | |
|---|---|---|
| adequate | conclude | inflammable |
| nourish | abolish | astonish |

7. Mom sprinkled a <u>fireproof</u> liquid over the stove. _____inflammable_____

8. Dad prepared a meal that could <u>starve</u> an army. _____nourish_____

9. The end of the movie will <u>bore</u> you. _____astonish_____

10. The candidate vowed to <u>create</u> high taxes. _____abolish_____

11. The game will <u>begin</u> when the final buzzer sounds. _____conclude_____

12. The detectives found <u>insufficient</u> information to name a suspect.
_____adequate_____

# WORD STUDY

**Prefixes** Write a sentence for each item. Use one word from the box in each sentence.

| | | |
|---|---|---|
| telephone | telecommunicate | telephoto |
| telescope | television | |

1. You are watching your favorite weekly show. You are sitting on the couch in your living room. Write a sentence to tell what you are doing.

_____ Sentence should include the word *television*. _____

2. You've heard that a comet is passing over your city. You go out on the back porch, but then you realize that you can't see the comet with your naked eye. Write a sentence to tell what you can use to see the comet.

_____ Sentence should include the word *telescope*. _____

3. You hear a ringing sound. Then you talk to your grandmother who lives in another town. Write a sentence to tell what you are using to talk to your grandmother.

_____ Sentence should include the word *telephone*. _____

4. Your friend has finally stood up on water skis! You want to take a picture to prove it, but you are onshore and your friend is in the middle of the lake. Write a sentence to tell how you will take the picture.

Sentence should include the word telephoto.

5. You think of something you want to tell your friend. But you're not allowed to talk on the phone this late. You can send an e-mail, though. Write a sentence to tell what you will do.

Sentence should include the word telecommunicate.

# CHALLENGE WORDS

## Word Learning—Challenge!

Study the spelling, part(s) of speech, and meaning(s) of each word. Complete each sentence by writing the word on the line. Then read the sentence.

1. **antiquated** *(adj.)* 1. out of date; 2. out of style

   The company's productivity was low because of _____antiquated_____ manufacturing methods.

2. **compile** *(v.)* 1. to collect and bring together; 2. to build up gradually

   Throughout the year, the teacher will _____compile_____ a book of the students' best writing samples.

3. **deficient** *(adj.)* lacking a needed element or quality

   A diet of ice cream would be _____deficient_____ in vitamins.

4. **dependent** *(adj.)* trusting or relying on another; *(n.)* one who relies on another for support

   The date of the picnic is _____dependent_____ on the weather.

   As long as you live at home, you will be a _____dependent_____ of your parents.

5. **saturate** *(v.)* 1. to fill completely; 2. to soak

   The heavy downpour will soon _____saturate_____ the ground.

# Use Your Vocabulary—Challenge!

*Here's What I Think!* The article that uses the Group B words on page 29 is an editorial. The writer wrote the article to express an opinion. On a separate sheet of paper, write your own editorial about an issue you feel strongly about. Use the Challenge Words below.

> antiquated      compile      deficient      dependent      saturate

## FUN WITH WORDS

Find and circle each word hidden in the puzzle below. Words may be horizontal, vertical, or diagonal. Some are spelled backwards.

> abolish      adequate      astonish      conclude      hoarse
>
> nourish      novel      prediction      scandal      traitor

```
L  J  U  H  T  V  O  U  S  C  A  M  S  L  A
A  A  D  E  Q  U  A  T  E  I  B  N  O  V  S
D  B  H  P  R  E  C  M  B  R  O  H  A  R  J
E  O  S  O  S  A  S  T  O  N  I  S  H  F  N
Q  L  I  B  A  R  N  E  K  O  W  Q  U  T  Y
L  I  R  N  U  G  K  R  O  P  J  K  D  E  E
S  S  U  A  R  G  U  I  G  O  L  T  H  D  D
B  H  O  A  R  S  E  V  X  S  D  E  L  Q  U
T  M  N  B  G  R  T  Y  U  J  M  L  V  L  L
P  R  E  D  I  T  Y  E  G  I  O  N  L  O  C
A  H  E  A  D  P  R  E  D  I  C  T  I  O  N
J  O  I  A  M  A  L  A  D  N  A  C  S  F  O
A  E  I  H  T  L  O  T  H  U  V  W  R  T  C
I  N  F  L  U  Y  G  T  R  A  I  T  O  R  S
```

# Review 1-3

## Word Meanings  Fill in the bubble of the word that is best defined by each phrase.

1. an object that circles a planet
   - **a.** treaty
   - **b.** scandal
   - **c.** satellite
   - **d.** molecule

2. relating to an essential characteristic of something
   - **a.** earnest
   - **b.** inherent
   - **c.** hoarse
   - **d.** perilous

3. one who betrays another
   - **a.** theory
   - **b.** solace
   - **c.** terrain
   - **d.** traitor

4. protection from destruction
   - **a.** compassion
   - **b.** salvation
   - **c.** circulation
   - **d.** charge

5. a seed vessel
   - **a.** pod
   - **b.** guppy
   - **c.** infection
   - **d.** conjunction

6. a serious statement
   - **a.** testimony
   - **b.** prediction
   - **c.** abuse
   - **d.** combat

7. a formal agreement between countries
   - **a.** terrain
   - **b.** mercy
   - **c.** circumference
   - **d.** treaty

8. to request help
   - **a.** appeal
   - **b.** accommodate
   - **c.** nourish
   - **d.** complicate

9. a reasonable explanation
   - **a.** charge
   - **b.** century
   - **c.** influence
   - **d.** theory

10. shocking behavior
    - **a.** migration
    - **b.** scandal
    - **c.** infantry
    - **d.** conjunction

11. overwhelming kindness and justice
    - **a.** channel
    - **b.** novel
    - **c.** mercy
    - **d.** pneumonia

12. easy to burn
    - **a.** inflammable
    - **b.** respectful
    - **c.** hoarse
    - **d.** influence

13. good enough
    - **a.** routine
    - **b.** earnest
    - **c.** novel
    - **d.** adequate

14. to treat badly or unkindly
    - **a.** abolish
    - **b.** abuse
    - **c.** harmonize
    - **d.** astonish

15. bits and pieces left after destruction
    - **a.** debris
    - **b.** mercy
    - **c.** prediction
    - **d.** terrain

# Sentence Completion

Choose the word from Part 1 that best completes each of the following sentences. Write the word in the blank. Then do the same for Part 2. You will not use all the words.

## Part 1

| routine | sanity | guarantee | inexpensive |
|---|---|---|---|
| ineffective | mentality | preserve | temptation |

1. I always have to fight the _____temptation_____ to ride my bicycle when I should be doing homework.

2. My bike is nothing fancy—just a(n) _____inexpensive_____ model—but I love to ride it in my neighborhood.

3. For me, a bicycle ride is never _____routine_____; it's always an adventure.

4. My mom says I like my bike so much that I have a "bicycling _____mentality_____."

5. I hope to _____preserve_____ my love of bikes throughout my life.

## Part 2

| annoy | furnished | earnest | accumulate |
|---|---|---|---|
| perilous | respectful | concluded | ambition |

6. My _____earnest_____ desire is to become a professional bicycle racer.

7. It can be _____perilous_____ work—some of the courses are risky and difficult.

8. When my mom heard that, she _____concluded_____ that she didn't want her daughter racing bikes.

9. Becoming a professional racer is my true _____ambition_____, so finally Mom said I can enter some of the beginners' races.

10. Eventually, I will _____accumulate_____ enough experience to move up to more advanced races.

# Synonyms

**Synonyms** Synonyms are words that have the same or nearly the same meanings. Choose the word from the box that is the best synonym for each group of words. Write your answer on the line.

| charge | migration | infection | ineffective | circulation |
|--------|-----------|-----------|-------------|-------------|
| conjunction | influence | abandon | complicate | |

1. movement, journey, travel _____ migration _____

2. leave, give up, forsake _____ abandon _____

3. association, joining _____ conjunction _____

4. disease, illness, plague _____ infection _____

5. distribution, rotation, flow _____ circulation _____

6. confuse, tangle, make more difficult _____ complicate _____

7. amount, fee; accuse, attack _____ charge _____

8. authority, control, power _____ influence _____

9. worthless, useless, weak _____ ineffective _____

# Antonyms

**Antonyms** Antonyms are words that have opposite or nearly opposite meanings. Choose the word from the box that is the best antonym for each group of words. Write your answer on the line.

| nourish | sanity | distract | compliment | combat |
|---------|--------|----------|------------|--------|
| abolish | novel | annoy | solace | |

1. focus, concentrate, emphasize _____ distract _____

2. typical, usual, familiar _____ novel _____

3. blame, disturb; grief, sadness _____ solace _____

4. poor mental health _____ sanity _____

**5.** leave in peace, not bother _____ annoy

**6.** insult, rude comment _____ compliment

**7.** peace, agreement _____ combat

**8.** starve, deprive, neglect _____ nourish

**9.** create, make, establish _____ abolish

# Word Riddles Choose the word from the box that answers the riddle. Write it on the line.

| astonish | guppy | respectful | century |
|---|---|---|---|
| molecule | prediction | harmonize | pneumonia |

**1.** I am a verb.
I mean "to surprise or amaze."
I am an antonym of *bore*.

I am _____ astonish _____.

**2.** I am a noun.
You might find me at a hospital.
I begin with a silent letter.

I am _____ pneumonia _____.

**3.** I am a noun.
You might find me in a science lab.
I am a tiny bit or particle.

I am _____ molecule _____.

**4.** I am a verb.
I am what people do when they
sing together.
I end with a suffix.

I am _____ harmonize _____.

**5.** I am a noun.
I rhyme with *affliction*.
I am a synonym of *forecast* or
*prognosis*.

I am _____ prediction _____.

**6.** I am a noun.
You might find me in your
aquarium.
I rhyme with *puppy*, but I don't walk
on a leash.

I am _____ guppy _____.

**7.** I am an adjective.
I describe your feeling for someone
you admire.
I end with a suffix.

I am _____ respectful _____.

**8.** I am a noun.
I'm often spoken of at a celebration.
I mean "a period of 100 years."

I am _____ century _____.

 **WORD LIST**

 **WORD STUDY**

Read each word using the pronunciation key.

## Group A

acquaint (ə kwānt´)
atmosphere (at´ məs fēr)
clarify (klâr´ ə fī)
conscience (kon´ shəns)
encounter (in koun´ tər)
homogenize (hə moj´ ə nīz)
nimble (nim´ bəl)
progress (n. prog´ res) (v. prə gres´)
scheme (skēm)
triumphant (trī um´ fənt)

## Group B

acquire (ə kwīr´)
annual (an´ yo͞o wəl)
classic (klas´ ik)
consist (kən sist´)
exceptional (ik sep´ shən əl)
injection (in jek´ shən)
nuisance (no͞o´ səns)
prompt (prompt)
security (si kyo͞or´ ə tē)
uncivilized (un siv´ ə līzd)

## Irregular Plurals

Plural words that do not end in *s* or *es* are called irregular plurals.

**bacteria** (bak tēr´ ē ə) microscopic living things *Singular:* **bacterium**

**brothers-in-law** (bruth´ ərz-in-lô) the brothers of a spouse or the husbands of sisters *Singular:* **brother-in-law**

**crises** (krī´ sēz) turning points *Singular:* **crisis**

**oxen** (oks´ ən) animals that are a kind of cattle *Singular:* **ox**

**teeth** (tēth) white, bonelike growths found in the mouth and used for chewing; projections *Singular:* **tooth**

**women** (wi´ mən) adult females of the human species *Singular:* **woman**

### Challenge Words

**devout** (di vout´)
**dwindle** (dwin´ dəl)
**exempt** (ig zempt´)
**impenetrable** (im pen´ i trə bəl)
**recur** (ri kər´)

*Level E*

■ **TEACHER TIP: See page ix for suggestions on how to use this page.**

# WORDS IN CONTEXT

Read each sentence below to figure out the meaning of the word in **bold.** Use reasoning skills and the remainder of the sentence to help you. Write the meaning of the word on the line.

1. Joshua gave a **triumphant** dance after scoring the touchdown.

   victorious

2. My little sister follows us around and makes a general **nuisance** of herself.

   pest

3. The doctor held up the needle and said, "This **injection** won't hurt a bit."

   shot

4. You have to be **nimble** to do skate tricks.

   agile

5. Kevin is always coming up with some clever **scheme** to help people.

   plot

6. Amanda's starring role showed that she was an **exceptional** actor for someone so young.

   outstanding

7. Pat is always **prompt** when he goes to a movie because he hates to miss the beginning.

   on time

8. A tour of the White House will **acquaint** you with important objects from our country's history.

   to introduce

9. Water **consists** of a combination of oxygen and hydrogen.

   to be made up of

10. It's always fun to go to art class because the **atmosphere** is informal and friendly.

    surrounding influence

# WORD MEANINGS

## Word Learning—Group A

Study the spelling, part(s) of speech, and meaning(s) of each word from Group A. Complete each sentence by writing the word on the line. Then read the sentence.

1. **acquaint** *(v.)* 1. to make known; 2. to inform; 3. to familiarize

   Take some time to _____acquaint_____ yourself with the new computers before you begin working.

2. **atmosphere** *(n.)* 1. the mass of air that surrounds the earth; 2. a surrounding influence

   Earth is the only known planet with an _____atmosphere_____ that supports life.

3. **clarify** *(v.)* 1. to make clear or easy to understand; 2. to explain

   This diagram will help _____clarify_____ the process for you.

4. **conscience** *(n.)* the sense within you that tells you when you are doing right or wrong

   Jeffrey had a guilty _____conscience_____ until he confessed his lie.

5. **encounter** *(v.)* 1. to meet by chance; 2. to be faced with; *(n.)* 1. an unexpected meeting; 2. a meeting of enemies

   Bailey was surprised to _____encounter_____ an acquaintance from home on her vacation in a distant state.

   Francisco's sudden _____encounter_____ with the large, friendly ape left him surprised but unhurt.

6. **homogenize** *(v.)* to blend different elements so they are evenly mixed

   To make milk more healthy to drink, the dairies _____homogenize_____ it before shipping it to the store.

7. **nimble** *(adj.)* 1. moving with agility; 2. active and sure-footed; 3. quick

   The _____nimble_____ goat easily hopped across the high, rocky hill without slipping or falling.

8. **progress** *(n.)* 1. movement toward a goal; 2. an advance; growth; *(v.)* 1. to move forward; 2. to proceed

   Kylie is making steady _____progress_____ in her study of Japanese.

   After a short delay for refueling, we were able to _____progress_____ on our journey across the continent.

9. **scheme** *(n.)* 1. a plan of action; 2. a plot

   If a money-making _____scheme_____ sounds too good to be true, it probably is.

10. **triumphant** *(adj.)* 1. victorious; 2. winning; 3. rejoicing for success at a victory

    We cheered as the players on the _____triumphant_____ team left the field.

## Use Your Vocabulary—Group A

Choose the word from Group A that best completes each sentence. Write the word on the line. You may use the plural form of nouns and the past tense of verbs if necessary.

Last night I dreamed I had a(n) __1__ with space creatures. I asked them about their background to better __2__ myself with these creatures. One creature explained that their __3__ was to land on the moon, but their spaceship had gotten off course. Sometimes I couldn't understand the creature's speech, so he drew a picture to __4__ what he said. Their mission was to learn how to __5__ their own dairy products—they'd heard that the moon was made of green cheese. After informing the aliens that grocery stores carry cheese, one creature made a __6__ leap high into the branches of a tree. He was surprised to learn that the gravity in the earth's __7__ made jumping so easy. We decided to go to the grocery store, but the weight of the spaceship in my truck made our __8__ slow. "Our mission is __9__!" the creatures yelled in unison. They left that night, but my __10__ still bothers me. I didn't tell them that the moon is not really made of cheese.

1. _____encounter_____
2. _____acquaint_____
3. _____scheme_____
4. _____clarify_____
5. _____homogenize_____
6. _____nimble_____
7. _____atmosphere_____
8. _____progress_____
9. _____triumphant_____
10. _____conscience_____

## Vocabulary in Action

The word *homogenize* can be used to talk about mixing many things. The best-known use of homogenization is in milk processing. Fresh, unprocessed milk separates on its own. The cream floats to the top, and water stays at the bottom. To keep milk from separating into water and cream, most dairies homogenize it. This explains why your first glass of rich, white milk will taste the same the next day too.

# Word Learning—Group B

Study the spelling, part(s) of speech, and meaning(s) of each word from Group B.
Complete each sentence by writing the word on the line. Then read the sentence.

1. **acquire** *(v.)* 1. to gain possession of something; 2. to get

    The museum director hoped to _____acquire_____ a famous painting at the auction.

2. **annual** *(adj.)* done or performed once a year; *(n.)* a plant that survives for one year or one season

    Chelsea can't wait for our _____annual_____ math competition.

    That _____annual_____ is so pretty that we will plant another one next spring.

3. **classic** *(adj.)* 1. of high value or quality; 2. excellent; 3. traditional; *(n.)* a work of great excellence

    The model with the huge fins is a _____classic_____ example of car design in the 1950s.

    That thrilling novel is a real _____classic_____.

4. **consist** *(v.)* to be made up of

    Doubleheaders _____consist_____ of two separate baseball games.

5. **exceptional** *(adj.)* 1. unusual; 2. varying from the norm

    The teacher's note says that Mya is an _____exceptional_____ math student.

6. **injection** *(n.)* the act or process of forcing liquid through a hollow needle

    The doctor gave Ashley an _____injection_____ of the vaccine.

7. **nuisance** *(n.)* a thing or person that is annoying or disagreeable

    A tiny mosquito can be a big _____nuisance_____.

8. **prompt** *(adj.)* on time; *(v.)* to move to action without delay

    Savanna sent a _____prompt_____ reply to my invitation.

    An alarm clock may _____prompt_____ Martin to get out of bed each day.

9. **security** *(n.)* 1. freedom from danger; 2. a feeling of being safe

    The return of their mother gave the lion cubs a sense of _____security_____.

10. **uncivilized** *(adj.)* 1. savage; 2. remote from settled areas

    Be sure to pack plenty of supplies if travelling in _____uncivilized_____ territory.

# Use Your Vocabulary—Group B

Choose the word from Group B that best completes each sentence. Write the word on the line. You may use the plural form of nouns and the past tense of verbs if necessary.

My father has a(n) __1__ 1925 Packard without a scratch on it. He __2__ the car five years ago from his friend. Dad keeps that car in __3__ condition. He parks it in a locked garage with a good __4__ system. Once a year, though, he takes the family to the __5__ antique car show in Detroit. You might think a car show would be a big mess, but think again. There is nothing __6__ about it. Everything is precisely planned. The show __7__ of three parts: the parade of cars, the judging and awarding of prizes, and an auction. One year we were late because we had to take our iguana to the vet for a(n) __8__. Since then, we've always been careful to be __9__. Towing the old Packard to Detroit can be a(n) __10__, but the show is so much fun that it's worth it!

1. _____ classic _____

2. _____ acquired _____

3. _____ exceptional _____

4. _____ security _____

5. _____ annual _____

6. _____ uncivilized _____

7. _____ consists _____

8. _____ injection _____

9. _____ prompt _____

10. _____ nuisance _____

# SYNONYMS

Synonyms are words that have the same or nearly the same meanings.

**Part 1** Choose the word from the box that is the best synonym for each group of words. Write the word on the line.

| | | | | |
|---|---|---|---|---|
| classic | homogenize | atmosphere | acquaint | scheme |
| clarify | consist | injection | uncivilized | encounter |

1. not settled, crude, wild _____ uncivilized _____

2. air; sense, surroundings _____ atmosphere _____

3. define, explain, interpret _____ clarify _____

4. high quality, traditional; masterpiece _____ classic _____

5. strategy, purpose, method _____ scheme _____

6. contain, include, involve         _____ consist _____

7. unexpected meeting; meeting of enemies      _____ encounter _____

8. shot, dose, treatment         _____ injection _____

9. introduce, tell, advise         _____ acquaint _____

10. mix, blend         _____ homogenize _____

**Part 2** Replace the underlined word(s) with a word from the box that means the same or almost the same. Write your answer on the line.

| acquire | annual | exceptional | prompt | nuisance |
|---------|--------|-------------|--------|----------|
| progress | nimble | security | triumphant | conscience |

11. Pedro hopes to <u>earn</u> enough money to get a new bike. _____ acquire _____

12. The school installed a new <u>protection</u> system. _____ security _____

13. We are planning our <u>yearly</u> vacation now. _____ annual _____

14. This graph shows the <u>growth</u> of the business last year. _____ progress _____

15. My <u>inner voice</u> warned me not to leave the job undone. _____ conscience _____

16. Miriam expected a <u>timely</u> answer to her question. _____ prompt _____

17. Guadalupe has an <u>outstanding</u> talent for drawing. _____ exceptional _____

18. Moses felt <u>successful</u> the first time he rode his rollerblades all the way down the hill without falling. _____ triumphant _____

19. Chores can be a <u>bother</u>, but they have to be done. _____ nuisance _____

20. The <u>graceful</u> dancer leaped high into the air. _____ nimble _____

## Vocabulary in Action

*Atmosphere* comes from the Latin words *atmos* (vapor) and *spharia* (sphere). When the word first appeared in English, people talked about it in reference to the air surrounding the moon. Later, scientists realized that the moon does not have an atmosphere. Today, many scientists believe the moon is surrounded by thin molecules. These molecules are similar to—but not exactly the same as—an atmosphere.

# ANTONYMS

Antonyms are words that have opposite or nearly opposite meanings.

**Part 1** Choose the word from the box that is the best antonym for each group of words. Write the word on the line.

| nuisance | nimble | triumphant |
|----------|--------|------------|
| exceptional | security | prompt |

1. beaten, defeated      _triumphant_

2. feeling of danger, risk, hazard      _security_

3. delight, pleasure, comfort      _nuisance_

4. tardy, late      _prompt_

5. clumsy, awkward, slow      _nimble_

6. common, ordinary, usual      _exceptional_

**Part 2** Replace the underlined word(s) with a word from the box that means the opposite or almost the opposite. Write your answer on the line.

| progress | uncivilized | acquire |
|----------|-------------|---------|
| clarify | classic | encounter |

7. The scientists planned to explore <u>settled</u> territory. _uncivilized_

8. Did my explanation <u>muddle</u> the situation? _clarify_

9. Wendy hopes to <u>avoid</u> her friend at the mall. _encounter_

10. Nickolas thinks my new song is <u>forgettable</u>. _classic_

11. Mom has said that we will <u>give up</u> more chores as we get older.
    _acquire_

12. My little sister hopes to <u>fall back</u> to a two-wheeler this spring.
    _progress_

### Notable Quotes

"Behold the turtle. He makes **progress** only when he sticks his neck out."

—James Bryant Conant (1893–1978), chemist, educator, politician

## WORD STUDY

**Irregular Plurals** Read each sentence. Then write a sentence that uses the plural form of the word in **bold**.

1. When I saw her from a distance, I didn't realize that the **woman** was my mother.

   *Sentence should include the word women.*

2. Bryant claims that he is as strong as an **ox**.

   *Sentence should include the word oxen.*

3. We looked at a one-celled **bacterium** under the microscope.

   *Sentence should include the word bacteria.*

4. When Keaton marries my sister Clara, I will have a new **brother-in-law**.

   *Sentence should include the word brothers-in-law.*

5. The dentist was able to save the **tooth** Ashton almost lost in the bicycle accident.

   *Sentence should include the word teeth.*

6. The first day of school may feel like a **crisis** to a kindergartner's parents.

   *Sentence should include the word crises.*

## CHALLENGE WORDS

### Word Learning—Challenge!

Study the spelling, part(s) of speech, and meaning(s) of each word. Complete each sentence by writing the word on the line. Then read the sentence.

1. **devout** *(adj.)* 1. earnest; 2. serious; 3. devoted to religion

   The _____devout_____ church members attended the meeting.

2. **dwindle** *(v.)* 1. to become less; 2. to shrink

   As our food supply began to _____dwindle_____, we anxiously waited for the snowplow's arrival.

3. **exempt** *(v.)* to release from a duty or rule; *(adj.)* free or released from a duty or rule

    The teacher promised to _____exempt_____ band members from the homework assignment on the night of the concert.

    In some states, food items are _____exempt_____ from a sales tax.

4. **impenetrable** *(adj.)* incapable of being pierced, entered, or passed

    Lesly warned us to avoid wandering into the _____impenetrable_____ forest.

5. **recur** *(v.)* 1. to be repeated; 2. to come up again for consideration

    The disease may _____recur_____ if you don't get enough rest.

## Use Your Vocabulary—Challenge!

*An Exceptional Experience* Think about an experience you've had or would like to have. Then write about your experience on a separate sheet of paper. You might write about a real experience, such as a trip to a car show, or a fantastic experience, such as an encounter with space aliens. Use the Challenge Words below.

| exempt | recur | impenetrable | dwindle | devout |
|--------|-------|--------------|---------|--------|

## FUN WITH WORDS

*Stranded!* You were out for a peaceful boat ride when a sudden storm forced you to abandon ship. Fortunately, you were able to struggle to shore on a deserted island. You have one bottle in which you can put a message telling what has happened and asking for help. Make your message clear and brief, but use at least eight of the words below.

| acquire | progress | uncivilized | encounter |
|---------|----------|-------------|-----------|
| consist | triumphant | nuisance | nimble |
| scheme | security | prompt | acquaint |

_____

_____

_____

_____

# CHAPTER 5

## WORD LIST

Read each word using the pronunciation key.

## Group A

acre (ā´ kər)
classify (klas´ ə fī)
contemplate (kon´ təm plāt)
explore (ik splôr´)
ideal (ī dēl´)
insane (in sān´)
numb (num)
protein (prō´ tēn)
sentimental (sen tə men´ təl)
unexpected (un ik spek´ tid)

## Group B

awkward (ôk´ wərd)
clot (klot)
contraction (kən trak´ shən)
export (v. eks pôrt´) (n. eks´ pôrt)
illustrate (il´ ə strāt)
intention (in ten´ shən)
orient (ôr´ ē ent)
pulse (puls)
seep (sēp)
vaccine (vak sēn´)

## WORD STUDY

### Prefixes

The prefix *mid-* means "in the middle of."

**midair** (mid âr´) not touching any surface
**midnight** (mid´ nīt) 12 o'clock at night
**midsize** (mid´ sīz) the size between large and small
**midterm** (mid turm´) halfway though a period of schooling
**midwinter** (mid´ win´ tər) halfway through the coldest season
**midyear** (mid´ yēr) halfway through a 12-month period

## Challenge Words

**antagonize** (an tag´ ə nīz)
**baffle** (baf´ əl)
**confederate** (kən fed´ ər it)
**corrode** (kə rōd´)
**vain** (vān)

**TEACHER TIP:** See page ix for suggestions on how to use this page.

*Level E*

# WORDS IN CONTEXT

Read each sentence below to figure out the meaning of the word in **bold**. Use reasoning skills and the remainder of the sentence to help you. Write the meaning of the word on the line.

1. Christopher is so **sentimental** that he cries while looking at his old photos.

   emotional

2. I noticed that water was beginning to **seep** through the crack in the pipe.

   to trickle

3. Sarah was taking a nap when an **unexpected** visitor knocked on the door.

   unplanned

4. **Vaccines** have wiped out many childhood diseases that were common only a few years ago.

   medicines

5. Neil Armstrong was one of the first Americans to **explore** the moon's surface.

   to investigate

6. The two words *can* and *not* can be combined to form the **contraction** *can't*.

   a shortening

7. My hands were **numb** after I got caught outdoors in snowy weather without my gloves.

   unfeeling

8. Before making her decision, the judge **contemplated** both sides of the issue.

   to have considered

9. I think it is an **insane** idea to dive into icy water in the middle of winter.

   extremely foolish

10. Thomas used a chart to **illustrate** how the accident happened.

    to explain with examples

# WORD MEANINGS

## Word Learning—Group A

Study the spelling, part(s) of speech, and meaning(s) of each word from Group A. Complete each sentence by writing the word on the line. Then read the sentence.

1. **acre** *(n.)* a unit of land equal to 43,560 square feet

   Each of the new houses will be built on an _____acre_____ of land.

2. **classify** *(v.)* to organize or arrange in groups or categories

   We plan to _____classify_____ these tree leaves and mount them in our science journals.

3. **contemplate** *(v.)* to think about or consider for a long time

   Before we panic, let's sit down and _____contemplate_____ the problem.

4. **explore** *(v.)* 1. to discover; 2. to investigate, study, or analyze

   Many people suffered great hardships in an effort to _____explore_____ the North Pole.

5. **ideal** *(n.)* 1. a standard of perfection; 2. a model to be imitated; 3. what one would want to be; *(adj.)* 1. existing as a mental image of perfection; 2. perfect

   Devin's dad is his _____ideal_____.

   A week on a tropical island would be my _____ideal_____ vacation.

6. **insane** *(adj.)* 1. crazy, mentally ill; 2. extremely foolish

   Climbing the tall tree to reach the window is an _____insane_____ idea.

7. **numb** *(adj.)* not having the power to feel or move normally; *(v.)* to dull the feelings of

   When Katherine first heard the news that her family would be moving, she was _____numb_____ with sadness.

   Before filling the tooth, the dentist will _____numb_____ your mouth.

8. **protein** *(n.)* a substance containing nitrogen that is a necessary part of animal and plant cells

   Paige suggested choosing a snack that is high in _____protein_____.

9. **sentimental** (*adj.*) 1. having or showing feeling; 2. acting from feelings rather than reason

   The old car is not worth much money, but it has _____ sentimental _____ value for the whole family.

10. **unexpected** (*adj.*) 1. unforeseen; 2. surprising; 3. startling

    The _____ unexpected _____ delay made us miss our next flight.

## Use Your Vocabulary—Group A

Choose the word from Group A that best completes each sentence. Write the word on the line. You may use the plural form of nouns and the past tense of verbs if necessary.

For a long time, my pals and I __1__ what we would do during spring vacation. Then Cassidy suggested that we go hiking in a nearby national park. We could probably __2__ several __3__ of the park in just one day. At first, we thought her idea was __4__. It sounded too difficult and tiring to us. But the more we thought about it, the more __5__ the trip began to sound. We planned carefully, filling our packs with water and a variety of snacks that were high in __6__. Mom suggested that we take a first-aid kit, just in case something __7__ happened. But nothing bad did happen. We enjoyed spending the whole day outdoors, and we met a friendly ranger who helped us __8__ the plants and animals we had seen. We walked until our feet were __9__, but we really had fun. We still feel __10__ when we remember that day.

1. _____ contemplated _____
2. _____ explore _____
3. _____ acres _____
4. _____ insane _____
5. _____ ideal _____
6. _____ protein _____
7. _____ unexpected _____
8. _____ classify _____
9. _____ numb _____
10. _____ sentimental _____

*Vocabulary in Action*

The word **vaccine** comes from the Latin word *vacca,* which means "cow." The first vaccine developed in the West was discovered by British physician Edward Jenner in 1796. Smallpox was a deadly disease that killed many people. Jenner discovered that people exposed to cowpox were immune to smallpox. Cowpox was similar to smallpox but weaker. Exposing people to cowpox made their bodies produce antibodies that protected them from smallpox. By 1977, vaccination programs such as those by the World Health Organization had eliminated smallpox worldwide.

## Word Learning—Group B

Study the spelling, part(s) of speech, and meaning(s) of each word from Group B.
Complete each sentence by writing the word on the line. Then read the sentence.

1. **awkward** *(adj.)* 1. clumsy; 2. lacking ease or grace when moving

   Tristan hates parties because he thinks he is an _____awkward_____ dancer.

2. **clot** *(n.)* a thick lump; *(v.)* to form into lumps

   The leftover gravy formed _____clots_____ on the plate as it cooled.

   The cut will stop bleeding as soon as the blood _____clots_____.

3. **contraction** *(n.)* 1. a drawing together; 2. a shortening or shrinking

   The painful cramp in his leg was caused by a muscle _____contraction_____.

4. **export** *(v.)* to send or carry goods out of one country for the use and sale in
   another; *(n.)* the act of carrying or removing something from a country

   The United States hopes to _____export_____ more goods in the future.

   The _____export_____ of native crafts is an important part of the small
   country's economy.

5. **illustrate** *(v.)* to make clear or explain by using stories or examples

   Liam went on to _____illustrate_____ his answer with examples from his own
   experience.

6. **intention** *(n.)* 1. a plan of action; 2. a purpose

   Malik has good _____intentions_____, but something always goes wrong.

7. **orient** *(v.)* 1. to place something so it faces a particular direction; 2. to adjust to a
   new situation or environment

   At first, Daisy found it difficult to _____orient_____ herself to the
   new school.

8. **pulse** *(n.)* any regular or measured beat or throb

   The rapid _____pulse_____ of the drums makes me feel like dancing.

9. **seep** *(v.)* to flow or pass slowly

   When the heavy snow melted, water began to _____seep_____ through
   the roof.

10. **vaccine** *(n.)* a preparation of dead or weakened germs of a particular disease that is
    given to a person to prevent or lessen effects of that disease

    Before starting school, most children are given a measles _____vaccine_____.

## Use Your Vocabulary—Group B

Choose the word from Group B that best completes each sentence. Write the word on the line. You may use the plural form of nouns and the past tense of verbs if necessary.

Avery decided to spend her vacation learning to be a volunteer at the local hospital. Her day began with a tour to help her **1** herself. Avery had many questions. She was afraid she might feel **2** around sick people, so an experienced volunteer gave her examples that **3** things she could say to patients. Avery comforted a child whose blood was beginning to **4** through a bandage. She explained that the blood would soon **5** and close the wound. She handed out juice to people who came in for their flu **6**, and a nurse showed her how to check the **7** of a person's artery. She wheeled a patient who was having a painful muscle **8** to the emergency room. At the end of the day, she toured the research lab, where chemists develop drugs that are **9** all over the world. Avery was thrilled with the whole day. She made up her mind then and there that it was her **10** to become a doctor.

1. _____ orient
2. _____ awkward
3. _____ illustrated
4. _____ seep
5. _____ clot
6. _____ vaccine
7. _____ pulse
8. _____ contraction
9. _____ exported
10. _____ intention

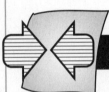

# SYNONYMS

Synonyms are words that have the same or nearly the same meanings.

**Part 1** Choose the word from the box that is the best synonym for each group of words. Write the word on the line.

| | | | | |
|---|---|---|---|---|
| insane | export | acre | classify | sentimental |
| pulse | protein | contraction | unexpected | ideal |

1. shipping, sending from; transport _____ export

2. sort, arrange, order _____ classify

3. reduction, shortening _____ contraction

**4.** mad, lunatic, foolish _____insane_____

**5.** perfect, best, model _____ideal_____

**6.** throb, regular beat, rhythm _____pulse_____

**7.** important part of plant and animal cells _____protein_____

**8.** a measured amount of land _____acre_____

**9.** emotional, not based on reason _____sentimental_____

**10.** abrupt, surprising, sudden _____unexpected_____

**Part 2** Replace the underlined word(s) with a word from the box that means the same or almost the same. Write your answer on the line.

| | | | | |
|---|---|---|---|---|
| contemplate | illustrate | clot | explore | awkward |
| numb | vaccine | seep | orient | intention |

**11.** It is Aaliyah's <u>plan</u> to practice all summer to make the soccer team.
_____intention_____

**12.** Blood is liquid in your veins, but it will <u>solidify</u> when it is exposed to air.
_____clot_____

**13.** If you are exposed to a <u>weakened form of a disease</u>, you are less likely to contract the full form of the disease. _____vaccine_____

**14.** The committee will <u>look into</u> our ideas for a new teen center.
_____explore_____

**15.** Andy put ice on the injury to <u>dull</u> the pain. _____numb_____

**16.** Air began slowly to <u>leak</u> out of the punctured tire. _____seep_____

**17.** We used a compass to <u>locate</u> ourselves during the long hike.
_____orient_____

**18.** Aesop told stories to <u>give examples of</u> the lessons he taught.
_____illustrate_____

**19.** The newborn colt's first steps were shaky and <u>ungraceful</u>. _____awkward_____

**20.** I promised to <u>ponder</u> my older sister's advice. _____contemplate_____

# ANTONYMS

Antonyms are words that have opposite or nearly opposite meanings.

> ideal       insane       contraction       numb

**Part 1** Choose the word from the box that is the best antonym for each group of words. Write the word on the line.

1. expansion, enlargement       _____contraction_____

2. right-minded, not crazy       _____insane_____

3. sensitive, able to move       _____numb_____

4. common, ordinary, imperfect       _____ideal_____

**Part 2** Replace the underlined word(s) with a word from the box that means the opposite or almost the opposite. Write your answer on the line.

> sentimental       awkward       unexpected       contemplate

5. Giraffes move with graceful strides. _____awkward_____

6. The council will probably ignore your comments. _____contemplate_____

7. The visit from Aunt Vickie was pretty normal. _____unexpected_____

8. As we threw away our old toys, we found ourselves being too practical.
_____sentimental_____

# WORD STUDY

**Prefixes** Use the words in the box to write a sentence for each item.

> midair       midyear       midwinter
>
> midnight       midsize       midterm

1. Write about something that would be fun to do late at night.

*Sentence should include the word midnight.*

**2.** Write about something you might buy that is not the largest or the smallest.

_____

Sentence should include the word *midsize.*

**3.** Write about the weather during the coldest part of the year.

_____

Sentence should include the word *midwinter.*

**4.** Write about something you do at school in the middle of the semester.

_____

Sentence should include the word *midterm.*

**5.** Write about something you will be doing when this year is half over.

_____

Sentence should include the word *midyear.*

**6.** Write about something that flies.

_____

Sentence should include the word *midair.*

 **CHALLENGE WORDS**

## Word Learning—Challenge!

Study the spelling, part(s) of speech, and meaning(s) of each word. Complete each sentence by writing the word on the line. Then read the sentence.

**1. antagonize** *(v.)* to create opposition or hostility

The fans' rude insults were meant to _____antagonize_____ the opposing team.

**2. baffle** *(v.)* 1. to bewilder; 2. to be too difficult for one to understand; 3. to confuse

Ciara's complicated ideas _____baffle_____ her friends.

**3. confederate** *(n.)* 1. an ally; 2. an accomplice

Dante admitted that he was a _____confederate_____ of the group who played the prank.

**4. corrode** *(v.)* to eat away slowly

Road salt will _____corrode_____ your car's body if you don't wash it off quickly.

**5. vain** *(adj.)* 1. having too much pride in one's looks or ability; 2. conceited

The other students soon tired of listening to Tony's ___vain___ boasts.

## Use Your Vocabulary—Challenge!

*My Spring Break* Plan ahead for a way to enjoy your next school break. On a separate sheet of paper, write about an idea for having fun or for learning something new. Use the Challenge Words below.

| vain | antagonize | confederate | corrode | baffle |
|------|------------|-------------|---------|--------|

# FUN WITH WORDS

Start in the middle of the maze. Use a pencil to draw a line from each word to its definition. You may find more than one way to get to the definition.

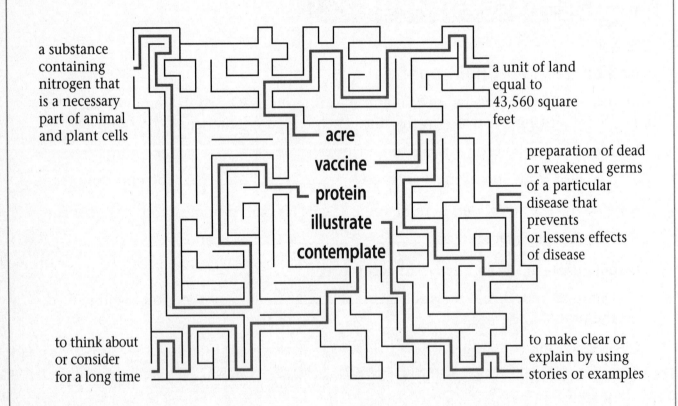

a substance containing nitrogen that is a necessary part of animal and plant cells

a unit of land equal to 43,560 square feet

acre
vaccine
protein
illustrate
contemplate

preparation of dead or weakened germs of a particular disease that prevents or lessens effects of disease

to think about or consider for a long time

to make clear or explain by using stories or examples

## WORD LIST

Read each word using the pronunciation key.

### Group A

**adjust** (ə just´)
**coarse** (kôrs)
**convention** (kən ven´ shən)

**forbidding** (fər bid´ iŋ)
**imperfect** (im pur´ fikt)
**irrigation** (ir ə gā´ shən)
**legislator** (lej´ is lāt ər)
**oblige** (ə blīj´)
**shellac** (shə lak´)
**squeamish** (skwēm´ ish)

### Group B

**administrator** (əd min´ ə strāt ər)
**compromise** (kom´ prə mīz)
**course** (kôrs)
**haggard** (hag´ ərd)
**irritate** (ir´ ə tāt)
**observe** (əb zurv´)
**ravine** (rə vēn´)
**sinister** (sin´ is tər)
**sterilize** (stâr´ ə līz)
**vault** (vôlt)

## WORD STUDY

### Analogies

An analogy is a comparison between different things. Read and study the following analogies. Decide how the words in each analogy are related.

**Sing** is to **song** as **read** is to **story.**

**Date** is to **calendar** as **time** is to **clock.**

**Rich** is to **wealthy** as **ill** is to **sick.**

## Challenge Words
**deflect** (di flekt´)
**deteriorate** (di tir´ ē ə rāt)
**devastate** (dev´ ə stāt)
**diffuse** (*adj.* di fyoos´) (*v.* di fyooz´)
**dissension** (di sen´ shən)

# WORDS IN CONTEXT

Read each sentence below to figure out the meaning of the word in **bold**. Use reasoning skills and the remainder of the sentence to help you. Write the meaning of the word on the line.

1. After Nicholas put a coat of **shellac** on the old oak desk, it looked as good as new.

   varnish
   _____

2. We sat quietly and **observed** the majestic bald eagles at the lake.

   watched
   _____

3. My brother **vaulted** over the fence and disappeared into the neighbor's yard.

   jumped
   _____

4. The noise of the vacuum cleaner **irritates** the baby.

   bothers
   _____

5. The **legislator** voted in favor of passing the new state law.

   lawmaker
   _____

6. The race **course** follows the river to the top of the hill.

   route
   _____

7. Alexis doesn't like that beach because the sand is too **coarse** and hurts her feet.

   rough
   _____

8. Dark, **sinister** clouds threatened rain during our picnic.

   menacing
   _____

9. After being lost in the mountains for days, the pilot looked **haggard** but happy when he was rescued.

   exhausted
   _____

10. Natalie attended a national **convention** for student newspaper editors.

    meeting
    _____

# WORD MEANINGS

## Word Learning—Group A

Study the spelling, part(s) of speech, and meaning(s) of each word from Group A.
Complete each sentence by writing the word on the line. Then read the sentence.

1. **adjust** *(v.)* 1. to adapt; 2. to become accustomed to

   It takes me about a week to _____adjust_____ to daylight saving time.

2. **coarse** *(adj.)* 1. not fine; 2. rough

   The blanket is made of a _____coarse_____ fabric that makes my skin itch.

3. **convention** *(n.)* an assembly of people meeting for some particular purpose

   José hoped he would be assigned to report on a political _____convention_____.

4. **forbidding** *(adj.)* 1. causing fear; 2. looking dangerous or unpleasant

   The growling polar bear looked so _____forbidding_____ I was glad there was a fence between us.

5. **imperfect** *(adj.)* not perfect; flawed

   Bryant's new glasses will correct his _____imperfect_____ vision.

6. **irrigation** *(n.)* a supplying of land with water

   In dry climates, farmers must build a system for _____irrigation_____ to water their crops.

7. **legislator** *(n.)* a member of a group that makes laws

   The voters' league keeps a record of how each _____legislator_____ votes.

8. **oblige** *(v.)* 1. to make a person thankful or grateful; 2. to require; 3. to do a favor for

   Joining the club will _____oblige_____ you to participate in at least three service projects.

9. **shellac** *(n.)* a type of varnish used as a wood filler and finish

   A sponge brush is a good tool for applying _____shellac_____.

10. **squeamish** *(adj.)* easily sickened

    Shelby gets _____squeamish_____ whenever she is around animals.

## Use Your Vocabulary—Group A

Choose the word from Group A that best completes each sentence. Write the word on the line. You may use the plural form of nouns and the past tense of verbs if necessary.

The life of a prospector was not for the __1__. It took time to __2__ to the Wild West. Prospectors never held a(n) __3__ to get together and share ideas. It was every person for himself! Prospectors would climb even the most __4__ mountains if they thought they'd find gold there. They would look for land that showed signs of good __5__. Then they would pan the __6__ sand in the streams to find gold nuggets. Even if they found some nuggets, __7__ ones weren't worth very much. Prospectors who staked a claim could put up a sign. They might even coat the sign with __8__ to keep the weather from washing off their name. But the prospectors had as much to fear from claim jumpers as the weather. The __9__ passed laws, but there was no one to enforce them. These daring adventurers were __10__ to look out for themselves.

1. _____ squeamish _____

2. _____ adjust _____

3. _____ convention _____

4. _____ forbidding _____

5. _____ irrigation _____

6. _____ coarse _____

7. _____ imperfect _____

8. _____ shellac _____

9. _____ legislators _____

10. _____ obliged _____

## Word Learning—Group B

Study the spelling, part(s) of speech, and meaning(s) of each word from Group B. Complete each sentence by writing the word on the line. Then read the sentence.

1. **administrator** *(n.)* a person who manages or directs

   The school _____ administrator _____ welcomed the students on the first day.

2. **compromise** *(v.)* to settle differences by agreeing that each side will give up part of what it demands

   Each group had to _____ compromise _____ to find a solution to the disagreement.

3. **course** *(n.)* 1. the route or direction taken by something; 2. a line of action; 3. a way of doing something; *(v.)* to flow quickly

   The sailor set a _____ course _____ toward home.

   The river's mighty waters _____ course _____ through the woods.

4. **haggard** *(adj.)* 1. looking worn, pale, and exhausted; 2. fatigued or worried

   We could tell by the firefighters' _____ haggard _____ faces that they had been battling the blaze all night.

5. **irritate** (*v.*) 1. to provoke impatience or anger; 2. to annoy

    Diana kept the speech short so as not to _____irritate_____ the audience.

6. **observe** (*v.*) 1. to watch; 2. to notice; 3. to show regard for

    Jalen and Jody often use a telescope to _____observe_____ the night sky.

7. **ravine** (*n.*) a long, deep, narrow valley usually worn down by running water

    Rocks and tree roots stuck out from both sides of the _____ravine_____.

8. **sinister** (*adj.*) 1. threatening; 2. evil; 3. dishonest

    The villain of the play had a _____sinister_____ grin.

9. **sterilize** (*v.*) to free from living germs

    Before we preserve the fruit, Mom must _____sterilize_____ the jars.

10. **vault** (*v.*) to jump or leap over something using some kind of support, such as a pole or the hands

    After spotting the bull, Kaleb hurried to _____vault_____ over the fence.

## Use Your Vocabulary—Group B

Choose the word from Group B that best completes each sentence. Write the word on the line. You may use the plural form of nouns and the past tense of verbs if necessary.

Some pioneers went west in search of land, not gold. They often went in wagon trains with a leader who acted as __1__. If the settlers looked __2__ at the end of their journey, it was because they faced many obstacles along their __3__. It was hard to get huge, clumsy wagons through deep __4__, and a team of oxen could not just __5__ over a mountain. Water might have to be __6__ before the thirsty travelers could take a drink. Sometimes a(n) __7__ person caused trouble on a wagon train. But usually trouble started because people were __8__ by traveling closely together for a long time. A wise leader __9__ the group very carefully. If he was able to head off trouble by suggesting acceptable __10__, the travelers made it safely to their new homes.

1. _____administrator_____

2. _____haggard_____

3. _____course_____

4. _____ravines_____

5. _____vault_____

6. _____sterilized_____

7. _____sinister_____

8. _____irritated_____

9. _____observed_____

10. _____compromises_____

# SYNONYMS

Synonyms are words that have the same or nearly the same meanings.

**Part 1** Choose the word from the box that is the best synonym for each group of words. Write the word on the line.

| observe | shellac | imperfect | squeamish | irritate |
|---------|---------|-----------|-----------|----------|
| coarse | legislator | sinister | irrigation | haggard |

1. easily ill, sensitive, delicate          squeamish

2. harmful, menacing, unkind          sinister

3. notice, watch; celebrate          observe

4. lawmaker, member of government          legislator

5. annoy, bother, pester          irritate

6. tired-looking, weary, gaunt          haggard

7. flawed, defective, unsound          imperfect

8. rough, scratchy, prickly          coarse

9. the watering of land          irrigation

10. varnish, polish          shellac

**Part 2** Replace the underlined word(s) with a word from the box that means the same or almost the same. Write your answer on the line.

| forbidding | course | adjust | sterilize | vault |
|------------|--------|--------|-----------|-------|
| oblige | compromise | convention | ravine | administrator |

11. Brook tries to <u>accommodate</u> her friends when they ask for a favor.
    _____oblige_____

12. Edgar's python looks <u>frightening</u>, but he is very gentle. _____forbidding_____

13. The caravan stayed on <u>the route</u> during the blizzard. _____course_____

14. The couple agreed to <u>meet halfway</u> to settle their quarrel. _____compromise_____

15. We learned a lot at the baseball card collectors' <u>conference</u>. _____convention_____

**16.** Geni found it hard to <u>adapt</u> to playing in the new league. _____ adjust _____

**17.** After each patient, the dentist must <u>disinfect</u> her instruments.
_____ sterilize _____

**18.** The muddy donkey climbed up the side of the <u>gorge</u>. _____ ravine _____

**19.** Every gymnast must learn to <u>spring</u> over the horse. _____ vault _____

**20.** The workers took their complaints to the <u>manager</u>. _____ administrator _____

 **ANTONYMS**

Antonyms are words that have opposite or nearly opposite meanings.

**Part 1** Choose the word from the box that is the best antonym for each group of words. Write the word on the line.

| squeamish | ravine | forbidding | compromise | observe |

**1.** neglect, pay no attention to _____ observe _____

**2.** mountain, peak _____ ravine _____

**3.** quarrel, contest, disagree _____ compromise _____

**4.** inviting, welcoming, pleasant _____ forbidding _____

**5.** not easily upset or sickened _____ squeamish _____

### Vocabulary in Action

The word *sinister* comes from a Latin word that means "on the left" or "unlucky." For many centuries, people who used their left hands were discouraged from doing so. Right-handed people were the majority, and they thought there was something wrong or unnatural about people who were left-handed. Luckily for left-handed people everywhere, this isn't the case in most of the world today. There are many examples of famous lefties—Benjamin Franklin, Bill Clinton, Helen Keller, Charlie Chaplin, Marie Curie, and Joan of Arc, to name just a few. Left-handers even have their own day. International Left-Handers Day is August 13.

**Part 2** Replace the underlined word with a word from the box that means the opposite or almost the opposite. Write your answer on the line.

> imperfect    coarse    sinister    irritated    haggard

6. The loud music from Chance's stereo <u>calmed</u> his mother. _____ irritated

7. Genesis looked <u>lively</u> the morning after her trip. _____ haggard

8. The painting is a <u>flawless</u> example of the Dutch style. _____ imperfect

9. The cheetah leaped to its feet and gave a <u>harmless</u> growl. _____ sinister

10. The <u>smooth</u> wool sweater is warm but scratchy. _____ coarse

## WORD STUDY

**Analogies** Select the word that completes each analogy.

1. **Color** is to **red** as **shape** is to _____.
   - a. scissors
   - b. blue
   - **c. square**
   - d. arithmetic

2. **Word** is to **book** as **ingredient** is to _____.
   - a. cook
   - **b. recipe**
   - c. mix
   - d. letter

3. **Attempt** is to **try** as **avoid** is to _____.
   - **a. escape**
   - b. awaken
   - c. greet
   - d. tempt

4. **Call** is to **shout** as **build** is to _____.
   - **a. construct**
   - b. demolish
   - c. telephone
   - d. hammer

5. **Morning** is to **afternoon** as **breakfast** is to _____.
   - a. eat
   - b. evening
   - c. cereal
   - **d. lunch**

**6.** **Foot** is to **ankle** as **hand** is to _____.

(a.) toe

(b.) finger

(c.) wrist

(d.) shake

 **CHALLENGE WORDS**

## Word Learning—Challenge!

Study the spelling, part(s) of speech, and meaning(s) of each word. Complete each sentence by writing the word on the line. Then read the sentence.

**1. deflect** *(v.)* to turn aside

Josue put up his hand to _____deflect_____ the snowball Elizabeth threw.

**2. deteriorate** *(v.)* to become worse in quality or value

These cheap shoes began to _____deteriorate_____ the first time I wore them.

**3. devastate** *(v.)* 1. to destroy; 2. to overwhelm

A tornado can _____devastate_____ a whole town in just a few minutes.

**4. diffuse** *(adj.)* 1. not concentrated; 2. scattered; *(v.)* to spread out

By the time we got there, the smoke was so _____diffuse_____ you could barely see it anymore.

The farmer made sure to _____diffuse_____ seeds to all parts of the field.

**5. dissension** *(n.)* 1. disagreement; 2. continuous quarreling

The umpire's call caused _____dissension_____ between the two teams.

## Use Your Vocabulary—Challenge!

*Time Machine* Of all the periods in our world's history, which one would you like to have lived in? Think about what life was like during that era and what you would be doing. On a separate sheet of paper, report on what you might see in that era. Use the Challenge Words above.

# FUN WITH WORDS

Use the clues to complete the puzzle. Choose from the words listed below. You will not use all the words.

| | | | | |
|---|---|---|---|---|
| compromise | ravine | oblige | convention | sinister |
| sterilize | shellac | squeamish | adjust | haggard |
| irritate | imperfect | course | observe | vault |

## Across

2. to settle an argument by agreeing that each side give up part of what it demands
6. to leap over something using a pole or hands
7. a long, deep, narrow valley usually worn by running water
8. threatening; evil
9. to watch and take note

## Down

1. to annoy
2. an assembly of people arranged for a particular purpose
3. made to feel sick easily
4. not perfect
5. to free from living germs
9. to do a favor for

The completed crossword puzzle:

Across:
2. COMPROMISE
6. VAULT
7. RAVINE
8. SINISTER
9. OBSERVE

Down:
1. IRRITATE
2. CONVENTION
3. SQUEAMISH
4. IMPERFECT
5. STERILIZE
9. OBLIGE

# Review 4-6

**Word Meanings** Fill in the bubble of the word that is best defined by each phrase.

1. to clear up
   - a. consist
   - b. explore
   - **c. clarify**
   - d. export

2. a plan of action
   - **a. scheme**
   - b. progress
   - c. protein
   - d. pulse

3. one time every year
   - **a. annual**
   - b. unexpected
   - c. numb
   - d. coarse

4. something that is a bother
   - a. atmosphere
   - b. injection
   - c. acre
   - **d. nuisance**

5. looking tired and worn out
   - a. awkward
   - b. sinister
   - **c. haggard**
   - d. squeamish

6. damaged, faulty
   - **a. imperfect**
   - b. nimble
   - c. classic
   - d. orient

7. scary, dangerous-looking
   - a. triumphant
   - **b. forbidding**
   - c. irritate
   - d. imperfect

8. absolutely perfect
   - a. insane
   - b. awkward
   - **c. ideal**
   - d. numb

9. to study carefully
   - **a. contemplate**
   - b. clot
   - c. encounter
   - d. compromise

10. to find out about
    - a. classify
    - **b. explore**
    - c. consist
    - d. illustrate

11. to mix together
    - a. sterilize
    - b. prompt
    - c. acquire
    - **d. homogenize**

12. to ooze
    - a. acquaint
    - **b. seep**
    - c. encounter
    - d. clot

13. to urge into action without delay
    - a. oblige
    - b. clarify
    - c. consist
    - **d. prompt**

14. the way something goes
    - a. coarse
    - b. scheme
    - **c. course**
    - d. security

15. out of the ordinary
    - a. uncivilized
    - b. sentimental
    - c. annual
    - **d. exceptional**

## Sentence Completion
Choose the word from Part 1 that best completes each of the following sentences. Write the word in the blank. Then do the same for Part 2. You will not use all the words.

### Part 1

| | | | |
|---|---|---|---|
| awkward | exceptional | prompted | conscience |
| acquire | observe | vaulted | orient |

1. The _____awkward_____ boy ran across the yard and crashed into a chair.

2. Cecilia ran down the field, placed the pole, and _____vaulted_____ ten meters up into the air.

3. _____Orient_____ the plants so that they face the sun.

4. Let's pack a picnic and _____observe_____ the fireworks display.

5. My _____conscience_____ told me I should not keep the wallet I found.

### Part 2

| | | | |
|---|---|---|---|
| acres | administrator | ravine | irrigation |
| export | adjust | vaccine | pulse |

6. We're going to _____export_____ this new computer game to countries around the world.

7. The pounding rain washed dirt and small rocks into the _____ravine_____.

8. They drove across Kansas and passed _____acres_____ of golden grain.

9. We've only lived here for two weeks, so I have not had time to _____adjust_____ to my new school.

10. Fifty years ago, everyone in the group was given a(n) _____vaccine_____ to prevent smallpox.

# Synonyms

**Synonyms** Synonyms are words that have the same or nearly the same meanings. Choose the word from the box that is the best synonym for each group of words. Write your answer on the line.

| unexpected | illustrate | irrigation | sterilize | nimble |
|---|---|---|---|---|
| security | clot | progress | oblige | |

1. the watering of land — irrigation
2. mass, clump; solidify, thicken — clot
3. move on, growth — progress
4. disinfect, purify, clean — sterilize
5. abrupt, surprising, sudden — unexpected
6. safety, protection, safeguard — security
7. spry, agile, graceful — nimble
8. give examples, clear up — illustrate
9. accommodate, help — oblige

# Antonyms

**Antonyms** Antonyms are words that have opposite or nearly opposite meanings. Choose the word from the box that is the best antonym for each group of words. Write your answer on the line.

| sentimental | insane | squeamish | contraction | encounter |
|---|---|---|---|---|
| compromise | irritate | classic | uncivilized | |

1. right-minded, not crazy — insane
2. not easily upset or sickened — squeamish
3. work of no value, of poor quality — classic
4. avoid, escape, retreat — encounter
5. calm, ease, comfort — irritate
6. expansion, enlargement — contraction
7. quarrel, contest, disagree — compromise

**8.** reasonable, realistic, practical        <u>sentimental</u>

**9.** refined, educated, settled        <u>uncivilized</u>

## Word Riddles  Choose the word from the box that answers the riddle. Write it on the line.

| administrator | injection | classify | triumphant |
|---|---|---|---|
| sinister | convention | acquire | intention |

**1.** I am a verb.

I am what you do when you sort laundry.
I am a synonym of *arrange*.

I am ____<u>classify</u>____.

**2.** I am a noun.

I begin with a prefix and end with a suffix.
I mean "a gathering of people meeting for a purpose."

I am ____<u>convention</u>____.

**3.** I am a noun.

I am something you plan to do.
I hope yours is good!

I am ____<u>intention</u>____.

**4.** I am a noun.

I am the person in charge.
I am a synonym of *director*.

I am ____<u>administrator</u>____.

**5.** I am a verb.

I rhyme with *desire*.
I am what you do when you get something.

I am ____<u>acquire</u>____.

**6.** I am an adjective.

I rhyme with *minister*.
But I am evil and menacing.

I am ____<u>sinister</u>____.

**7.** I am a noun.

You may not want me, but I'm good for you.
I end in a suffix.

I am ____<u>injection</u>____.

**8.** I am an adjective.

I am the way you feel when you are successful.
I am an antonym of *defeated*.

I am ____<u>triumphant</u>____.

# WORD LIST

Read each word using the pronunciation key.

## Group A

absolute (ab sə lo͞ot´)
abundant (ə bun´ dənt)
admirable (ad´ mər ə bəl)
criticize (krit´ i sīz)
frame (frām)
impure (im pyo͝or´)
issue (ish´ yo͞o)
recall (v. ri kôl´) (n. rē´ kôl)
stern (stərn)
vertebra (vər´ tə brə)

## Group B

aggressive (ə gres´ iv)
boast (bōst)
comment (kom´ ent)
cultivate (kul´ tə vāt)
fraud (frôd)
incident (in´ si dənt)
kerosene (ker´ ə sēn)
reclaim (ri klām´)
strive (strīv)
victorious (vik tôr ē əs)

# WORD STUDY

## Suffixes

The suffix -*ship* means "a state or quality of being" or "the art or skill of."

**authorship** (ô´ thər ship) the profession of a writer

**championship** (cham´ pyən ship) a game or contest that determines an overall winner

**friendship** (frend´ ship) an amicable relationship

**kinship** (kin´ ship) the connection between family members

**scholarship** (skol´ ər ship) knowledge attained by studying

**sportsmanship** (spôrts´ mən ship) fair and honest behavior

## Challenge Words

**expenditure** (ik spen´ di chər)
**fastidious** (fa stid´ ē əs)
**gaudy** (gô´ dē)
**humility** (hyo͞o mil´ i tē)
**paltry** (pôl´ trē)

■ **TEACHER TIP:** See page ix for suggestions on how to use this page.    *Level E*

Read each sentence below to figure out the meaning of the word in **bold**. Use reasoning skills and the remainder of the sentence to help you. Write the meaning of the word on the line.

1. The **stern** expression on my mother's face let me know she was angry because I was late.

   strict
   _____

2. We remembered to bring **kerosene** for our camp stove, but we forgot the matches.

   fuel oil
   _____

3. Divers went down to see whether the ancient shipwreck could be **reclaimed.**

   recovered
   _____

4. Andrew's friends soon tired of listening to him **boast** about his new bike.

   to brag
   _____

5. Her face was familiar, but I could not **recall** her name.

   to remember
   _____

6. The **victorious** tennis team held a party to celebrate winning the tournament.

   winning
   _____

7. Afterward, we realized we should not have **criticized** Hailey's decision to quit the basketball team.

   found fault with
   _____

8. Dr. Hunter's claim that his potion could make people fly was discovered to be a **fraud.**

   deception
   _____

9. "Our company," declared the president, "will continue to **strive** to find new ways to improve our service."

   to try hard
   _____

10. Melissa did not want her **comments** to be misunderstood, so she took the time to explain herself carefully.

    remarks
    _____

*Chapter 7   Level E*

# WORD MEANINGS

## Word Learning—Group A

Study the spelling, part(s) of speech, and meaning(s) of each word from Group A. Complete each sentence by writing the word on the line. Then read the sentence.

1. **absolute** *(adj.)* 1. complete; 2. not limited in any way

   Before testifying, Cole swore to tell the _____ absolute _____ truth.

2. **abundant** *(adj.)* more than enough

   The settlers prepared an _____ abundant _____ supply of food for the winter.

3. **admirable** *(adj.)* 1. worth admiring; 2. very good; 3. excellent

   Jorge has so many _____ admirable _____ talents.

4. **criticize** *(v.)* 1. to find fault with; 2. to consider the good and bad points of something and judge accordingly

   After the movie, my friends and I gathered to _____ criticize _____ it.

5. **frame** *(v.)* 1. to lie to make an innocent person appear guilty; 2. to shape; 3. to construct; *(n.)* something composed of parts fitted together

   The accused man said that others wanted to _____ frame _____ him.

   The builders began by putting up the _____ frame _____ of the house.

6. **impure** *(adj.)* 1. not pure; 2. mixed with something of a lesser value

   That ring is inexpensive because it is made of _____ impure _____ gold.

7. **issue** *(v.)* 1. to send out; 2. to put forth; *(n.)* a matter that is in dispute between two or more people

   The police chief promised to _____ issue _____ a statement about the arrest.

   The students asked the counselor to help them settle the _____ issue _____.

8. **recall** *(v.)* 1. to call back to mind; 2. to remember; *(n.)* a call to return something

   It's fun to _____ recall _____ the good times we had last summer.

   The car manufacturer issued a _____ recall _____ because some of the air bags were slow to inflate.

9. **stern** *(adj.)* severe; strict; harsh

   The general is a fair but _____ stern _____ leader.

10. **vertebra** *(n.)* one of the bones that makes up the backbone

    Veronica fractured a _____ vertebra _____ when she fell from her skateboard.

## Use Your Vocabulary—Group A

Choose the word from Group A that best completes each sentence. Write the word on the line. You may use the plural form of nouns and the past tense of verbs if necessary.

For 50 years, Preston had bought every stamp __1__ by the post office. He had a(n) __2__ collection. His __3__ supply of stamps filled his whole house, and Preston could easily __4__ every stamp he owned. One day Preston came home and discovered that the glass case he had once __5__ to protect his most valuable stamp was unlocked. He was filled with complete and __6__ terror. The stamp was gone! He heard a creak, and every muscle along each __7__ of his back tightened. Preston called out, "Halt!" in a(n) __8__ voice. He raced down the hall and saw a figure limp quickly away. Suddenly Preston felt like his invaded home was dirty and __9__. His hand shook as he dialed the police. At that moment, no one would have __10__ Preston for his angry thought: "I hope that rotten thief gets what he deserves!"

1. _____ issued _____
2. _____ admirable _____
3. _____ abundant _____
4. _____ recall _____
5. _____ framed _____
6. _____ absolute _____
7. _____ vertebra _____
8. _____ stern _____
9. _____ impure _____
10. _____ criticized _____

## Word Learning—Group B

Study the spelling, part(s) of speech, and meaning(s) of each word from Group B. Complete each sentence by writing the word on the line. Then read the sentence.

1. **aggressive** *(adj.)* 1. making the first move in an attack or a quarrel; 2. attacking

    Slowly back away from an _____ aggressive _____ alligator.

2. **boast** *(v.)* to speak of oneself or what one owns with excessive pride

    Ashlyn tried not to _____ boast _____ about her new car too often.

3. **comment** *(n.)* a note or remark expressing opinion or attitude; *(v.)* to make a note or remark

    Trenton was cheered by the coach's encouraging _____ comment _____.

    The reporter invited people to _____ comment _____ on the new law.

4. **cultivate** *(v.)* 1. to help plants grow by working and caring for them; 2. to improve by labor, care, or study

    It takes lots of hard work to _____ cultivate _____ a rose garden.

**5. fraud** (*n.*) 1. someone who is not what he or she pretends to be; 2. deception

The investigator gathered enough evidence to expose the _____fraud_____.

**6. incident** (*n.*) 1. a happening or an occurrence; 2. something dependent on something of greater importance

Because of the _____incident_____ in the gym, two players were suspended.

**7. kerosene** (*n.*) a thin oil made from petroleum and used as fuel for lamps, stoves, and engines

We lit the cabin with lamps that burned _____kerosene_____.

**8. reclaim** (*v.*) 1. to bring back to a useful, good condition; 2. to rescue from an undesirable state

We can _____reclaim_____ this overgrown garden with hard work.

**9. strive** (*v.*) to work or try hard

Jed promised that he would _____strive_____ to improve his grades.

**10. victorious** (*adj.*) 1. having won a victory; 2. of or relating to victory; 3. successful

The crowd stood and cheered for the _____victorious_____ athlete.

## Use Your Vocabulary—Group B

Choose the word from Group B that best completes each sentence. Write the word on the line. You may use the plural form of nouns and the past tense of verbs if necessary.

Police Sergeant Conner answered the call. He listened without **1** to Preston's story and then said, "I hate to **2** , but in my 20 years, I have solved every case." Sergeant Conner promised to **3** to solve this case too. From the beginning, he took a(n) **4** approach. He **5** his interest in stamps. After he had learned all he could, he read the new police reports. He read about a(n) **6** in which a suspicious character posing as a stamp expert had tried to sell a rare stamp to a stamp dealer. Sergeant Conner arranged to be at the shop the next day. He had the dealer pretend the power had failed and lit **7** lamps. Then Conner hid in the shadows. When the thief came in, the sergeant shouted, "I arrest you for **8** !" He **9** Preston's stamp and was **10** once again.

1. _____comment_____
2. _____boast_____
3. _____strive_____
4. _____aggressive_____
5. _____cultivated_____
6. _____incident_____
7. _____kerosene_____
8. _____fraud_____
9. _____reclaimed_____
10. _____victorious_____

# SYNONYMS

Synonyms are words that have the same or nearly the same meanings.

**Part 1** Choose the word from the box that is the best synonym for each group of words. Write the word on the line.

| | | | | |
|---|---|---|---|---|
| issue | recall | reclaim | admirable | incident |
| absolute | criticize | impure | aggressive | vertebra |

1. remember; a request to give back        __recall__

2. hostile, bold, charging        __aggressive__

3. unclean, not filtered        __impure__

4. judge, not approve of        __criticize__

5. distribute, give out; problem, dispute        __issue__

6. episode, event, occasion        __incident__

7. wonderful, worthy of praise        __admirable__

8. total, thorough, whole        __absolute__

9. a bone in the back        __vertebra__

10. take back, restore, recover        __reclaim__

## Vocabulary in Action

*Vertebra* comes from the Latin word *vertere*, which means "to turn." Other words that come from this word include *verse, vertigo, introvert,* and *anniversary*. Find these words in a dictionary. Do you see how each word includes some kind of "turn"?

**Part 2** Replace the underlined word with a word from the box that means the same or almost the same. Write your answer on the line.

| | | | | |
|---|---|---|---|---|
| fraud | kerosene | comments | boast | strive |
| stern | frame | abundant | cultivate | victorious |

11. Abraham made a few very smart <u>observations</u> about the novel.

     __comments__

**12.** The <u>structure</u> of the new house will be made of steel, not wood.
_____frame_____

**13.** The swindler is going to jail for committing a <u>deception</u>. _____fraud_____

**14.** We ask only that you always <u>attempt</u> to play your best chess game.
_____strive_____

**15.** We lit the <u>oil</u> in our antique lamps. _____kerosene_____

**16.** Mallory earns excellent grades, but she does not <u>brag</u> about them.
_____boast_____

**17.** The sergeant's <u>tough</u> words stirred the soldiers to action. _____stern_____

**18.** The farmer began to <u>plant</u> her crops in early spring. _____cultivate_____

**19.** The <u>triumphant</u> hockey team will take home the trophy. _____victorious_____

**20.** A <u>plentiful</u> feast was prepared for the workers. _____abundant_____

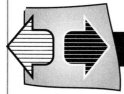 **ANTONYMS**

Antonyms are words that have opposite or nearly opposite meanings.

**Part 1** Choose the word from the box that is the best antonym for each group of words. Write the word on the line.

| strive | fraud | victorious |
|--------|-------|------------|
| reclaim | stern | abundant |

**1.** truth, good faith, honesty _____fraud_____

**2.** destroy, make unusable _____reclaim_____

**3.** goof off, be lazy _____strive_____

**4.** insufficient, scarce, not enough _____abundant_____

**5.** defeated, beaten, overcome _____victorious_____

**6.** permissive, soft, easygoing _____stern_____

**Part 2** Replace the underlined word(s) with a word from the box that means the opposite or almost the opposite. Write your answer on the line.

| | | |
|---|---|---|
| aggressive | criticize | recall |
| impure | admirable | issue |

7. The board member took time to <u>praise</u> the new policy. _____criticize_____

8. The police officer said he had to <u>take back</u> a ticket. _____issue_____

9. We felt light-headed after breathing all that <u>wholesome</u> air. _____impure_____

10. I can't seem to <u>forget</u> my awful first experience at summer camp.

_____recall_____

11. Pierce spent the weekend engaged in <u>terrible</u> activities. _____admirable_____

12. Daron is too <u>shy</u> to be successful as a sales representative. _____aggressive_____

## WORD STUDY

**Suffixes** Read each story. Write the word from the box that names the story's theme.

| | | |
|---|---|---|
| friendship | scholarship | kinship |
| championship | authorship | sportsmanship |

1. With two outs in the last inning, the Eagles were ahead by one run. Yesenia pitched a high fastball. Crack! A home run. It was all over for the Eagles. Yesenia felt like crying, but she forced herself to smile as she passed the opponent's bench. "Congratulations," she said. "You played a great game!"

_____sportsmanship_____

2. Every morning, Zackary goes into his office and turns on the computer. Even if he's tired or has a bad day, he forces himself to write at least one page of his novel. One day, he will see his novel on the library shelf.

_____authorship_____

3. Albert and Fabian like to spend time together. When Fabian is sad, Albert cheers him up. When Fabian gets something new, he can't wait to share it with Albert. They hope their relationship will last forever.

_____friendship_____

4. Each year the Washington family holds a reunion. Babies are introduced, and the families share stories. Cousins remember how much fun it is to be together. All the Washingtons value their time together.

_____ kinship _____

5. Kassandra spends lots of time studying. She is the first member of her family to go to college. Her grades put her at the top of her class. She studies hard not only to keep up her grades. She knows that if she studies hard enough, she can find an alternative to gasoline and change the world.

_____ scholarship _____

6. Tabitha has competed in a dozen chess tournaments. This year, though, she is the second-ranked player in her division. She has spent the entire weekend playing against her opponents. She has defeated all the lower-ranked players. There is only one player left to beat. He is the top-ranked player. Tabitha plans to take home that trophy this year, and Devonte Charles is not going to stop her!

_____ championship _____

## CHALLENGE WORDS

## Word Learning—Challenge!

Study the spelling, part(s) of speech, and meaning(s) of each word. Complete each sentence by writing the word on the line. Then read the sentence.

1. **expenditure** *(n.)* 1. spending; 2. the amount of time, energy, or money spent

    Ramon realized that another ____expenditure____ was not in his budget.

2. **fastidious** *(adj.)* 1. difficult to please; 2. fussy or picky

    Gina is ____fastidious____ about the placement of every object in her room.

3. **gaudy** *(adj.)* cheap; showy; tasteless

    I liked the outfit, but Shaun said it was too ____gaudy____.

4. **humility** *(n.)* 1. lack of arrogance; 2. meekness

    ____Humility____ is an appealing quality in a star athlete.

5. **paltry** *(adj.)* almost worthless

    Viviana thought the job was worth more than that ____paltry____ sum.

# Use Your Vocabulary—Challenge!

*It's a Mystery* Do you think you would make a good detective? On a separate sheet of paper, try writing a mystery story for practice. Tell about the crime and the solution. Use the Challenge Words below.

> expenditure    fastidious    gaudy    humility    paltry

# FUN WITH WORDS

An *anagram* is a word made by mixing up the letters of one word in order to spell another word. For example, rearranging the letters of the word *moat* gives us the anagram *atom*. The letters are the same; they're just in a different order.

In the challenge below, you'll see an equation like this:

**Example: seeker + no = an oily seeker** _____

The letters to the left of the equal sign are an anagram of a vocabulary word (plus one or two additional letters that are needed to complete the word). The words to the right of the equal sign give you a hint. In the sample above, combine the letters from the word *seeker* with the letters *no* and rearrange them. You should come up with *kerosene*, a word that describes a type of oil. Write the vocabulary word in the blank.

1. bats + o = you can brag about your bats _____ boast

2. rent + s = this rent is very serious _____ stern

3. prime + u = this anagram should be cleaned _____ impure

4. earl + lc = do you remember this earl? _____ recall

5. moment + c = at this moment, I must speak _____ comment

6. camel + ir = I want my camel back! _____ reclaim

7. rebate + vr = watch your back on this one _____ vertebra

8. tables + ou = truly complete tables _____ absolute

9. lattice + uv = make this lattice grow _____ cultivate

10. alarmed + ib = this is an excellent alarm _____ admirable

# WORD LIST

Read each word using the pronunciation key.

## Group A

alarm (ə lärm´)
buff (buf)
common (kom´ ən)
frontier (frun tēr´)
incidental (in si den´ təl)
legend (lej´ ənd)
manacle (man´ ə kəl)
orbit (ôr´ bit)
reduce (ri do͞os´)
vivid (viv´ id)

## Group B

bureau (byo͝or´ ō)
commotion (kə mō´ shən)
deliberately (di lib´ ər it lē)
genuine (jen´ yo͝o in)
inconsiderate (in kən sid´ ər it)
magnificent (mag nif´ i sənt)
parasite (pâr´ ə sīt)
reign (rān)
suppress (sə pres´)
survey (sər vā´)

# WORD STUDY

## Root Words

The root *scribe* means "write."

ascribe (ə skrīb´) to credit to; to attribute to

describe (di skrīb´) to tell or write about

inscribe (in skrīb´) to write a person's name on a list; to write a short message in a book

prescribe (prē skrīb´) to write an order for medicine; to give advice

proscribe (prō skrīb´) to forbid

subscribe (səb skrīb´) to sign an agreement for a product or service; to give approval to

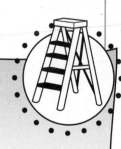

## Challenge Words

brusque (brusk)
dexterity (dek ster´ i tē)
incessant (in ses´ ənt)
peerless (pēr´ lis)
pompous (pom´ pəs)

© Loyola Press.

■ TEACHER TIP: See page ix for suggestions on how to use this page.

# WORDS IN CONTEXT

Read each sentence below to figure out the meaning of the word in **bold**. Use reasoning skills and the remainder of the sentence to help you. Write the meaning of the word on the line.

1. This summer I plan to **reduce** the amount of time I spend watching TV.

   to decrease

2. The sheriff placed a **manacle** on the prisoner's wrists to prevent his escape.

   handcuff

3. It's obvious that Jessica did not **deliberately** break the glass.

   purposely

4. The **reign** of the beloved queen continued for many years.

   period of power

5. The smoke from Joseph's science experiment set off the fire **alarm.**

   signal

6. Alexandra tried to **suppress** her urge to giggle during her sister's recital.

   to smother

7. Jordan loves to wax the car, and she will **buff** it over and over until it gleams.

   to polish

8. As the satellite follows its **orbit** around the earth, it sends back valuable weather information.

   circular path

9. Everyone was delighted by the food at the **magnificent** banquet.

   wonderful

10. The museum curator proved that the newly found painting was a **genuine** work by Picasso.

   authentic

# WORD MEANINGS

## Word Learning—Group A

Study the spelling, part(s) of speech, and meaning(s) of each word. Complete each sentence by writing the word on the line. Then read the sentence.

1. **alarm** *(v.)* to make afraid or frighten; *(n.)* 1. sudden fear; 2. a signal that warns people

   "I don't mean to _____alarm_____ you," Jackson said, "but you are about to sit on a bumblebee."

   The class formed an orderly line at the sound of the fire _____alarm_____.

2. **buff** *(v.)* to polish or shine; *(n.)* soft, orange-yellow leather used for polishing

   Ask someone at the auto body shop to _____buff_____ out that scratch on your fender.

   Ian carefully polished the car with a clean, new _____buff_____.

3. **common** *(adj.)* 1. general; 2. usual; 3. having no special position; 4. belonging to all in a group

   All the members of the chess club shared a _____common_____ interest.

4. **frontier** *(n.)* 1. the last edge of developed country; 2. a border between countries

   Life on the _____frontier_____ held many hardships for the pioneers.

5. **incidental** *(adj.)* occurring by chance

   The two friends were pleased by their _____incidental_____ meeting.

6. **legend** *(n.)* 1. a story coming down from the past that may or may not be based on fact; 2. an explanatory list of symbols on a chart

   The story of Paul Bunyan is an American folk _____legend_____.

7. **manacle** *(n.)* something used to bind or secure a wrist; a handcuff

   The prisoner was secured by a _____manacle_____ on each arm.

8. **orbit** *(n.)* the circular path of an object around another object, usually in space

   Earth travels in an _____orbit_____ around the sun.

9. **reduce** *(v.)* 1. to make smaller; 2. to decrease

   Every day Kaylee tries to _____reduce_____ the amount of time it takes her to run a mile.

10. **vivid** *(adj.)* 1. having the appearance of freshness; 2. in colors, very strong

    The _____vivid_____ colors of the sunset were reflected in the lake.

## Use Your Vocabulary—Group A

Choose the word from Group A that best completes each sentence. Write the word on the line. You may use the plural form of nouns and the past tense of verbs if necessary.

Oral historians travel around the country collecting old songs and  1 . Some of the best can be traced back to the pioneers who settled the western  2 . According to one story, attacks by bandits and wild animals were so  3  that the pioneers didn't even blink when it happened. But even the bravest pioneer was  4  by the thought of an attack by the ferocious half-bear, half-horse beast called Krakakatoe. To  5  the possibility of a surprise attack, the settlers hired Big Dallas Dawes to protect them. One night Dallas stayed up late to  6  his new sheriff's badge. As he walked out into the moonlight to see if the badge was shiny enough, he had a(n)  7  meeting with the slobbering, howling Krakakatoe. Dazzled by the bright glare of the badge, the monster stopped short. Dallas quickly attached a(n)  8  to the monster's wrist and tied his lasso to it. Then he swung the rope—and the monster—above his head and hurled it clear into  9 . And the monster is there still. Have you ever heard a(n) 10  howl in the night? That's the Krakakatoe flying overhead.

1. _____ legends _____

2. _____ frontier _____

3. _____ common _____

4. _____ alarmed _____

5. _____ reduce _____

6. _____ buff _____

7. _____ incidental _____

8. _____ manacle _____

9. _____ orbit _____

10. _____ vivid _____

### Vocabulary in Action

The word **manacle** has the same Latin root as several other English words including *manifest* and *emancipate*. Its Latin root *manus* means "hand." The word *manacle* first appeared around the year 1306.

# Word Learning—Group B

Study the spelling, part(s) of speech, and meaning(s) of each word from Group B.
Complete each sentence by writing the word on the line. Then read the sentence.

1. **bureau** *(n.)* 1. a chest of drawers, sometimes with a mirror; 2. a division of a government department

   Mom folded the T-shirts and placed them in a drawer in the baby's _____bureau_____.

2. **commotion** *(n.)* 1. a violent movement; 2. confusion; 3. disturbance

   A cougar caused a _____commotion_____ at the barbecue.

3. **deliberately** *(adv.)* 1. on purpose; 2. after careful and thorough consideration

   Mikayla explained that she had not picked up the wrong backpack _____deliberately_____.

4. **genuine** *(adj.)* 1. actual; 2. true; 3. sincere; 4. honest

   It appears that the party was a _____genuine_____ surprise to Ariana.

5. **inconsiderate** *(adj.)* careless of others and their feelings, thoughtless

   Margaret apologized for making an _____inconsiderate_____ remark that hurt Edward's feelings.

6. **magnificent** *(adj.)* grand; splendid; impressive

   Isabelle wore _____magnificent_____ jewelry to the dance.

7. **parasite** *(n.)* a living thing that spends its life on or in another, which it usually injures

   Because the tree had been invaded by some kind of _____parasite_____, we had to cut it down.

8. **reign** *(n.)* the period of power of a ruler; royal authority; *(v.)* to rule

   The _____reign_____ of Henry VIII was filled with scandals.

   Erik already knew he was next in line to _____reign_____ over his country.

9. **suppress** *(v.)* 1. to put an end to; 2. to hold in or back; 3. to stop with force

   Troops were sent to the town to _____suppress_____ the rebellion.

10. **survey** *(v.)* 1. to examine; 2. to inspect

    The president flew over the area in a helicopter to _____survey_____ the flood damage.

## Use Your Vocabulary—Group B

Choose the word from Group B that best completes each sentence. Write the word on the line. You may use the plural form of nouns and the past tense of verbs if necessary.

An international research team, sent to __1__ a remote region of Mochea, made an important discovery. Among the ancient ruins, the team found a statue of a Royal Mountain leech, an extinct __2__ that disappeared hundreds of years ago. The researchers thought that the statue was an artifact from the __3__ of Queen Xalia, the greatest ruler of ancient Mochea. With its gold casting and brilliant colors, the statue was a valuable and __4__ piece of art. The researchers shipped the statue to the International __5__ of Ancient Civilizations for further study. When it arrived, the golden leech created quite a(n) __6__ among the experts. Thorough testing confirmed that the statue was indeed __7__. The researchers were thrilled. They wanted to claim the statue, but the Mochean government asked that it be returned. At first, some members of the team planned to __8__ ignore the request. But they soon realized that they had to __9__ their dishonest and __10__ desires for history's sake. Today the statue is back in the country that has been its home for hundreds of years.

1. _____ survey _____

2. _____ parasite _____

3. _____ reign _____

4. _____ magnificent _____

5. _____ Bureau _____

6. _____ commotion _____

7. _____ genuine _____

8. _____ deliberately _____

9. _____ suppress _____

10. _____ inconsiderate _____

# SYNONYMS

Synonyms are words that have the same or nearly the same meanings.

**Part 1** Choose the word from the box that is the best synonym for each group of words. Write the word on the line.

| | | | | |
|---|---|---|---|---|
| alarm | frontier | deliberately | reduce | magnificent |
| inconsiderate | incidental | suppress | parasite | genuine |

1. rude, thoughtless, insensitive _____ inconsiderate _____

2. purposefully, in an unhurried way _____ deliberately _____

3. real, authentic, proven, pure _____ genuine _____

4. scare, panic; alert, fear _____ alarm _____

5. lessen, shrink, diminish _____ reduce _____

6. overcome, stop, smother _____ suppress _____

7. edge, boundary _____ frontier _____

8. wonderful, fine, superb _____ magnificent _____

9. thing that lives in or on another _____ parasite _____

10. unplanned, accidental _____ incidental _____

**Part 2** Replace the underlined word(s) with a word from the box that means the same or almost the same. Write your answer on the line.

| orbit | vivid | buff | reign | commotion |
|-------|-------|------|-------|-----------|
| survey | legend | manacle | bureau | common |

11. The community members worked toward a public goal. _____ common _____

12. Look over the headings and questions before you read. _____ survey _____

13. The slave broke the shackle and escaped to freedom. _____ manacle _____

14. The engineers sighed with relief as the satellite settled into its pathway around the earth. _____ orbit _____

15. The antique cabinet filled one whole wall of the room. _____ bureau _____

16. It's fun to sit around a campfire and tell an old story. _____ legend _____

17. The arrival of the movie star caused an uproar at the mall. _____ commotion _____

18. Mercedes had to polish her shoes until her face was reflected in them. _____ buff _____

19. The bright colors in the painting attracted my attention. _____ vivid _____

20. The new queen promised to govern with kindness and fairness. _____ reign _____

# ANTONYMS

Antonyms are words that have opposite or nearly opposite meanings.

**Part 1** Choose the word from the box that is the best antonym for each group of words. Write the word on the line.

| | | |
|---|---|---|
| deliberately | commotion | common |
| suppress | incidental | vivid |

1. continue, express, let out      _suppress_

2. peace, calm, quiet      _commotion_

3. dull, colorless, pale      _vivid_

4. impulsively, suddenly, quickly      _deliberately_

5. not usual, private, secret      _common_

6. planned, occurring on purpose      _incidental_

**Part 2** Replace the underlined word(s) with a word from the box that means the opposite or almost the opposite. Write your answer on the line.

| | | |
|---|---|---|
| genuine | reduce | alarmed |
| magnificent | frontier | inconsiderate |

7. I liked Lindsay right away because of her insincere smile.      _genuine_

8. We were calmed when we heard the TV weather bulletin.      _alarmed_

9. The family planned to build a new life in the settled region.
     _frontier_

10. It's a good idea to increase the amount of sugar in our diet.
     _reduce_

11. We all gathered on the porch to gaze at the ordinary rainbow.
     _magnificent_

12. The other children found Sergio's comments thoughtful.      _inconsiderate_

# WORD STUDY

**Root Words** Add a prefix from the box to the root to make a word that fits each clue. Then write a sentence using the word.

| a- | de- | in- | pre- | pro- | sub- |

1. An action that is forbidden by law is _____pro_____ scribed.

   _Sentence should include the word proscribed._

2. A rumor can be _____a_____ scribed to the person who began it.

   _Sentence should include the word ascribed._

3. You can sign a contract to _____sub_____ scribe to your favorite magazine.

   _Sentence should include the word subscribe._

4. A doctor may _____pre_____ scribe medicine to treat an illness.

   _Sentence should include the word prescribe._

5. Before you give a book as a gift, you may want to _____in_____ scribe a message on the inside front cover.

   _Sentence should include the word inscribe._

6. A person who told what something looks like has _____de_____ scribed it.

   _Sentence should include the word described._

# CHALLENGE WORDS

## Word Learning—Challenge!

Study the spelling, part(s) of speech, and meaning(s) of each word. Complete each sentence by writing the word on the line. Then read the sentence.

1. **brusque** _(adj.)_ 1. abrupt; 2. blunt

   Calvin's _____brusque_____ answer discouraged the reporter from asking any more questions.

2. **dexterity** _(n.)_ skill and ease in using the hands, mind, or body

   April handles her skateboard with amazing _____dexterity_____.

**3. incessant** *(adj.)* continuing without interruption

The child's _____incessant_____ snoring kept the whole family awake.

**4. peerless** *(adj.)* 1. without a match; 2. without an equal

The _____peerless_____ skater won the gold medal easily.

**5. pompous** *(adj.)* 1. arrogant; 2. acting too proudly

The audience walked out on the _____pompous_____ and long-winded speaker.

## Use Your Vocabulary—Challenge!

*Tell the Tale* Stories such as the legend of Krakakatoe are called tall tales. American pioneers told tall tales around a campfire after a day of grueling travel. What other tall tales do you know? On a separate sheet of paper, create a new tall tale that describes another adventure Big Dallas Dawes might have had. Use the Challenge Words below.

| brusque | dexterity | incessant | peerless | pompous |

# FUN WITH WORDS

King Ragnama wants you to join the quest for the Golden Dictionary. But first you must pass a final test to prove your worthiness. Answer each of King Ragnama's questions below.

1. Name two things that *alarm* you.

   Answers will vary.
   _____

2. Name one *genuine* act of kindness you have performed recently.

   Answers will vary.
   _____

3. Describe the most *magnificent* thing you have ever seen.

   Answers will vary.
   _____

4. Parts of the kingdom are not yet settled. Would you be willing to journey to the *frontier*? Why or why not?

   Answers will vary.
   _____

5. Would you agree to travel with an *inconsiderate* but very strong person? Why or why not?

   Answers will vary.
   _____

 **WORD LIST**

Read each word using the pronunciation key.

## Group A

- **caravan** (kâr´ ə van)
- **competition** (kom pi tish´ ən)
- **destination** (des tə nā´ shən)
- **indigo** (in´ də gō)
- **magnify** (mag´ nə fī)
- **mutual** (myoō´ choō əl)
- **parliament** (pär´ lə mənt)
- **relate** (ri lāt´)
- **survival** (sər vī´ vəl)
- **wedge** (wej)

## Group B

- **cell** (sel)
- **compensation** (kom pən sā´ shən)
- **completion** (kəm plē´ shən)
- **disassemble** (dis ə sem´ bəl)
- **greedily** (grēd´ i lē)
- **industry** (in´ də strē)
- **remedy** (rem´ i dē)
- **revolt** (ri vōlt´)
- **tactics** (tak´ tiks)
- **yearn** (yərn)

 **WORD STUDY**

## Prefixes

The prefix *sub-* means "under."

- **subfreezing** (sub frē´ ziŋ) below a temperature of 32° Fahrenheit
- **submarine** (sub´ mə rēn) something that lives or operates underwater
- **submerge** (səb mərj´) to place underwater
- **subsoil** (sub´ soil) the layer of dirt under the topsoil
- **substandard** (sub stan´ dərd) inferior to or different from the norm
- **subway** (sub´ wā) an underground passage or railway

### Challenge Words

- **confirm** (kən fərm´)
- **conflict** (*n.* kon´ flikt) (*v.* kən flikt´)
- **defer** (di fər´)
- **precipitate** (pri sip´ i tāt)
- **steep** (stēp)

■ TEACHER TIP: See page ix for suggestions on how to use this page.

*Level E*

# WORDS IN CONTEXT

Read each sentence below to figure out the meaning of the word in **bold**. Use reasoning skills and the remainder of the sentence to help you. Write the meaning of the word on the line.

1. Taylor offered Daniel 10 dollars as **compensation** for mowing her lawn.

   payment
   _____

2. At the bonfire, Savannah **related** stories about her travels in Mongolia.

   told
   _____

3. The unhappy peasants united to plan a **revolt** against the wicked king.

   mutiny
   _____

4. Kyle **greedily** ate all the best snacks before the guests arrived.

   selfishly
   _____

5. After the photo had been **magnified**, the detective was able to spot a clue that helped her solve the mystery.

   enlarged
   _____

6. As soon as the concert ended, workers began to **disassemble** the portable stage.

   to take down
   _____

7. Freezing temperatures and hungry polar bears make **survival** in the Arctic very difficult.

   staying alive
   _____

8. **Tactics** such as whining and crying will not make Christina change her mind.

   methods
   _____

9. As soon as the Andersons reach their **destination**, they plan to check in, change, and jump into the swimming pool.

   journey's end
   _____

10. Garrett and Kelly have a **mutual** interest in punk rock records.

    shared
    _____

# WORD MEANINGS

## Word Learning—Group A

Study the spelling, part(s) of speech, and meaning(s) of each word from Group A.
Complete each sentence by writing the word on the line. Then read the sentence.

1. **caravan** *(n.)* a group of people traveling together, often through dangerous areas

   As the _____ caravan _____ headed west, the onlookers cheered and waved.

2. **competition** *(n.)* 1. the act of two or more people independently trying to win or gain something; 2. a contest

   Unfortunately, the tennis _____ competition _____ was postponed due to rain.

3. **destination** *(n.)* the place a person or thing is being sent

   Be sure to leave early enough to reach your _____ destination _____ on time.

4. **indigo** *(n.)* a blue dye that can be obtained from various plants

   Before making the shawl, Riley colored her yarn with _____ indigo _____ .

5. **magnify** *(v.)* to cause objects to appear larger than they really are

   We had to _____ magnify _____ the bacteria with the microscope before we were able to see them.

6. **mutual** *(adj.)* 1. having similar or shared feelings; 2. given and received

   By _____ mutual _____ agreement, Alexis and Summer decided to never quarrel again.

7. **parliament** *(n.)* the highest lawmaking body in some countries

   Nolan hopes to be elected to _____ parliament _____ someday.

8. **relate** *(v.)* 1. to give an account of; 2. to tell; 3. to show a connection between

   Josiah was invited to _____ relate _____ stories of his childhood.

9. **survival** *(n.)* 1. the act of surviving; 2. living or continuing longer than others

   The _____ survival _____ of a species depends upon its ability to change over time.

10. **wedge** *(n.)* a piece of wood or metal that tapers to a thin edge

    Marco placed a _____ wedge _____ under the door to keep it from closing.

## Use Your Vocabulary—Group A

Choose the word from Group A that best completes each sentence. Write the word on the line. You may use the plural form of nouns and the past tense of verbs if necessary.

Would you like me to __1__ the story of our class trip? The __2__ was Ottawa, the capital of Canada. Our __3__ of three buses started out while it was still dark. The sky looked as if it had been dyed with __4__. As the sun rose, we spotted a flock of geese. They were flying in a formation shaped like a(n) __5__ and were heading the same way we were. We were all wide awake, so we decided to have a singing __6__. Each side of the bus tried to drown out the other. Finally, our teachers begged us to stop. They claimed it was life or death, a matter of __7__, but you know how teachers are. They seem to __8__ every little thing. In Ottawa, we had lunch and then watched members of __9__ at work. By the time we climbed back in the buses to go home, we were almost as tired as our teachers. By __10__ agreement, we decided to sleep all the way home.

1. _____relate_____

2. _____destination_____

3. _____caravan_____

4. _____indigo_____

5. _____wedge_____

6. _____competition_____

7. _____survival_____

8. _____magnify_____

9. _____parliament_____

10. _____mutual_____

## Word Learning—Group B

Study the spelling, part(s) of speech, and meaning(s) of each word from Group B. Complete each sentence by writing the word on the line. Then read the sentence.

1. **cell** (n.) extremely small unit of living matter that makes up all living things

   In biology class, we identified the parts of a plant _____cell_____.

2. **compensation** (n.) 1. something given to someone to make up for something else; 2. an equivalent; 3. pay

   Peyton didn't want _____compensation_____ for his volunteer work.

3. **completion** (n.) 1. finishing; 2. the act of being finished or done

   The school will celebrate the _____completion_____ of the new library.

4. **disassemble** (v.) to take apart

   The historical society plans to _____disassemble_____ the old log cabin and rebuild it in the city park.

5. **greedily** (adv.) acting with a strong desire to have a lot of something

   As the guests arrived, Ava _____greedily_____ grabbed each present.

6. **industry** *(n.)* 1. all such business, manufacture, and trade taken as a whole;
   2. manufacturing as a whole; 3. steady effort

   Adrianna plans to train for a career in the automotive _____industry_____.

7. **remedy** *(v.)* to cure; *(n.)* a treatment that relieves or cures a disease

   My plan will _____remedy_____ the crowding problems in the lunchroom.

   Six patients volunteered to test the new cold _____remedy_____.

8. **revolt** *(n.)* the act of rebelling; *(v.)* to turn and fight against a leader

   The _____revolt_____ of the colonists led to the birth of the United States.

   The tyrant didn't think his subjects would _____revolt_____ against him.

9. **tactics** *(n.)* 1. ways or methods to gain advantage; 2. ways to accomplish an end

   The president approved of General Clark's _____tactics_____.

10. **yearn** *(v.)* 1. to feel a longing or desire; 2. to feel tenderness

    A month of snowy days made Lauren _____yearn_____ for summer.

## Use Your Vocabulary—Group B

Choose the word from Group B that best completes each sentence. Write the word on
the line. You may use the plural form of nouns and the past tense of verbs if necessary.

When I took the babysitting job, I expected to
spend a quiet evening studying for my biology
test on __1__ while little Trey slept. Instead I had
to cope with a preschooler who was in __2__. Trey
was as destructive as the whole demolition __3__ put
together. First, he tried to __4__ the TV remote
control. When I turned my back, he broke into
a "childproof" cabinet and __5__ ate a whole box
of cookies. No matter what __6__ I tried, I couldn't
seem to __7__ the situation. It wasn't long before I
was beginning to __8__ for the job's __9__. I swore that
no amount of __10__ would make me sit for Trey
ever again. But then little Trey crawled into my
lap. "You're my favorite babysitter," he said sweetly.
Maybe I will try it one more time.

1. _____cells_____

2. _____revolt_____

3. _____industry_____

4. _____disassemble_____

5. _____greedily_____

6. _____tactics_____

7. _____remedy_____

8. _____yearn_____

9. _____completion_____

10. _____compensation_____

## SYNONYMS

Synonyms are words that have the same or nearly the same meanings.

**Part 1** Choose the word from the box that is the best synonym for each group of words. Write the word on the line.

| | | | | |
|---|---|---|---|---|
| yearn | indigo | destination | wedge | parliament |
| compensation | remedy | disassemble | relate | survival |

1. heal, treat; cure, medicine      remedy

2. want, long for, desire      yearn

3. living, staying alive, lasting      survival

4. target, goal, journey's end      destination

5. dismantle, take down, break up      disassemble

6. pie-shaped piece of wood or metal      wedge

7. reward, fee, payback      compensation

8. lawmaking body      parliament

9. blue dye      indigo

10. report, speak, tell      relate

**Part 2** Replace the underlined word(s) with a word from the box that means the same or almost the same. Write your answer on the line.

| | | | | |
|---|---|---|---|---|
| cell | greedily | competition | mutual | completion |
| caravan | tactics | industry | revolt | magnify |

11. Tatiana and Elise became friends because of their <u>shared</u> interests.
     mutual

12. The <u>procession</u> of trucks formed a long line on the highway.      caravan

13. Members of the computer <u>business</u> attended a convention.      industry

14. The <u>rebellion</u> ended when the dictator fled the country.      revolt

15. If we <u>enlarge</u> the picture, we might see our faces in the crowd.
     magnify

**16.** Some creatures only have one living unit of matter. _____ cell

**17.** Allen used underhanded methods to convince people to give him their money. _____ tactics

**18.** We cheered as our ferret won the ugly pet contest at the fair. _____ competition

**19.** The baby birds chirped hungrily in the nest. _____ greedily

**20.** If you pass the class, you will receive a certificate of finishing. _____ completion

# ANTONYMS

Antonyms are words that have opposite or nearly opposite meanings.

**Part 1** Choose the word from the box that is the best antonym for each group of words. Write the word on the line.

| | | |
|---|---|---|
| survival | revolt | magnify |
| mutual | compensation | completion |

**1.** cause to look smaller _____ magnify

**2.** death, extermination, extinction _____ survival

**3.** loss, expense _____ compensation

**4.** starting, beginning _____ completion

**5.** one-sided, separate _____ mutual

**6.** obey, give loyalty to; support _____ revolt

## Vocabulary in Action

The word **magnify** first appeared in the English language around 1380. At that time, it meant "to praise" or "to speak of the glory of something or someone." In older translations of the Bible, you can still find the phrase "magnify the Lord." This doesn't mean "to make God bigger." The meaning of the word has changed. *Magnify* first meant "to cause objects to appear larger than they really are" around 1665, almost 300 years after the word surfaced in English.

**Part 2** Replace the underlined word(s) with a word from the box that means the opposite or almost the opposite. Write your answer on the line.

| | | |
|---|---|---|
| yearn | remedy | disassemble |
| destination | relate | competition |

7. The doctor prescribed a <u>poison</u> to treat the disease. ___remedy___

8. The hikers reached their <u>starting point</u> by sunset. ___destination___

9. The <u>cooperation</u> between the candidates was incredible. ___competition___

10. Saul had to <u>build</u> a car engine before he could understand how it worked. ___disassemble___

11. Her long travels on boats and trains made Miranda <u>hate</u> to sleep at home again. ___yearn___

12. My older sister loves to <u>keep secret</u> tales of my childhood. ___relate___

# WORD STUDY

**Prefixes** Use two words from the box to answer each question.

| | | |
|---|---|---|
| submarine | subfreezing | submerge |
| subsoil | substandard | subway |

1. What might happen if a contractor built a building on a patch of ground with an underground stream running through it?

    _Sentence should include the words substandard and subsoil._

2. What might happen if a criminal tried to dispose of a weapon by throwing it into a pond when the temperature has been below 32° Fahrenheit for a month?

    _Sentence should include the words submerge and subfreezing._

3. What is the difference between a ride in a vehicle that travels underwater and a ride in a vehicle that travels underground?

    _Sentence should include the words submarine and subway._

# CHALLENGE WORDS

## Word Learning—Challenge!

Study the spelling, part(s) of speech, and meaning(s) of each word. Complete each sentence by writing the word on the line. Then read the sentence.

1. **confirm** *(v.)* 1. to prove true; 2. to give approval

   The scientists planned a series of experiments that would finally either _____confirm_____ or disprove their theory.

2. **conflict** *(n.)* 1. a fight; 2. lack of agreement; *(v.)* to strongly disagree

   The _____conflict_____ began with a misunderstanding.

   Ryan's opinions _____conflict_____ with those of Paola.

3. **defer** *(v.)* 1. to put off; 2. to postpone; 3. to give in to an opinion

   Ezekiel had to _____defer_____ his vacation until the busy season was over.

4. **precipitate** *(v.)* 1. to bring about abruptly; 2. to condense as water vapor that then falls in the form of rain or snow

   The confusion over the boundary may _____precipitate_____ a crisis between the two countries.

5. **steep** *(adj.)* having a sharp angle or slope; *(v.)* to soak in a liquid

   Waves crashed against the _____steep_____ cliff.

   Before cooking the meat, Linda will _____steep_____ it overnight in her special sauce.

## Use Your Vocabulary—Challenge!

***All in a Day's Work***   Have you ever had a babysitting job or another type of job? What was hard about it? What was fun? On a separate sheet of paper, write about a job you have had or would like to have. Use the Challenge Words above.

You have found the Golden Dictionary of Spelrix! You must discover the secret phrase that will unlock the book. Match the vocabulary words with the definitions below. Write one letter of the word in each blank. Use the numbered letters to find out the secret phrase at the bottom of the page, and the Golden Dictionary will be yours!

1. ways to accomplish an end   T   A   C   T   I   C   S
                                       1

2. continuing longer than others   S   U   R   V   I   V   A   L
                                        2

3. a treatment for a disease   R   E   M   E   D   Y
                                            3

4. to make something appear larger   M   A   G   N   I   F   Y
                                                  4

5. a lawmaking body   P   A   R   L   I   A   M   E   N   T
                                              5

6. acting with a desire to have a lot   G   R   E   E   D   I   L   Y
                                                         6

7. all of manufacturing   I   N   D   U   S   T   R   Y
                                              7

8. money received for work   C   O   M   P   E   N   S   A   T   I   O   N
                                                    8

9. to long for   Y   E   A   R   N
                     9

10. a V-shaped piece of wood   W   E   D   G   E
                                   10

11. having feelings that are alike   M   U   T   U   A   L
                                                    11

12. a blue dye   I   N   D   I   G   O
                                 12

Secret phrase:   A   L   W   A   Y   S       C   H   O   O   S   E
                 11  6  10  11  9   8       1      12  12  8   5

    Y   O   U   R       W   O   R   D   S       W   I   S   E   L   Y   .
    9   12  2   7      10  12  7   3   8       10  4   8   5   6   9

# Review 7–9

**Word Meanings** Fill in the bubble of the word that is best defined by each phrase.

1. true and sincere
   a. incidental   **b. genuine**   c. abundant   d. aggressive

2. a group of lawmakers
   **a. parliament**   b. revolt   c. frontier   d. industry

3. to make useful again
   a. suppress   b. caravan   **c. reclaim**   d. manacle

4. a list that explains symbols on a map or chart
   a. incident   b. fraud   c. bureau   **d. legend**

5. an oil used as fuel
   **a. kerosene**   b. cell   c. parasite   d. orbit

6. to show how one thing connects to another
   a. yearn   **b. relate**   c. strive   d. issue

7. a blue dye made from certain plants
   a. remedy   b. vertebra   **c. indigo**   d. compensation

8. to shrink
   a. buff   b. recall   c. reclaim   **d. reduce**

9. strict and hard
   a. inconsiderate   b. aggressive   **c. stern**   d. impure

10. ways to get something
    a. destination   **b. tactics**   c. comment   d. survival

11. to study carefully
    **a. survey**   b. cultivate   c. revolt   d. criticize

12. a backbone
    **a. vertebra**   b. indigo   c. wedge   d. competition

13. done or said after careful thought
    **a. deliberately**   b. mutual   c. greedily   d. genuine

14. to make a steady effort
    a. frame   **b. strive**   c. disassemble   d. cultivate

15. very brightly colored
    a. admirable   b. common   **c. vivid**   d. victorious

# Sentence Completion

Choose the word from Part 1 that best completes each of the following sentences. Write the word in the blank. Then do the same for Part 2. You will not use all the words.

## Part 1

| | | | |
|---|---|---|---|
| alarm | commotion | bureau | mutual |
| remedy | suppress | frame | absolute |

1. Allie built the _____ frame _____ of the birdhouse first.

2. Cara decided that only the _____ absolute _____ quiet of the library would help her concentrate.

3. Let's not _____ alarm _____ the citizens with crazy rumors.

4. The people causing all the _____ commotion _____ outside made Guillermo look up from his book.

5. The doctor has just found a(n) _____ remedy _____ for the patient's mysterious illness.

## Part 2

| | | | |
|---|---|---|---|
| wedge | revolt | magnify | common |
| reign | completion | magnificent | comment |

6. The audience cheered wildly at the _____ magnificent _____ display of fireworks.

7. Elian whittled the block of wood until he had made a _____ wedge _____ for the door.

8. The critic praised the new play, but he made a negative _____ comment _____ about the silly costumes.

9. The young king did his best to _____ reign _____ over his subjects firmly but fairly.

10. Scientists used a microscope to _____ magnify _____ the red blood cells and make them visible to the eye.

## Synonyms
Synonyms are words that have the same or nearly the same meanings. Choose the word from the box that is the best synonym for each group of words. Write your answer on the line.

| abundant | buff | competition | caravan | orbit |
|---|---|---|---|---|
| revolt | common | cultivate | incident | |

1. course, pathway, circuit      orbit

2. rebellion; mutiny, rise up against      revolt

3. plant, farm, develop, nurture      cultivate

4. ordinary, plain, public      common

5. episode, event, occasion      incident

6. match, contest      competition

7. plentiful, more than enough      abundant

8. rub, brighten; a type of leather      buff

9. band, procession, fleet      caravan

## Antonyms
Antonyms are words that have opposite or nearly opposite meanings. Choose the word from the box that is the best antonym for each group of words. Write your answer on the line.

| completion | victorious | recall | survival | impure |
|---|---|---|---|---|
| incidental | frontier | mutual | aggressive | |

1. death, extermination, extinction      survival

2. interior, settled region      frontier

3. defeated, beaten, overcome      victorious

4. planned, occurring on purpose      incidental

5. peaceful, shy, friendly      aggressive

6. clean, wholesome, unpolluted      impure

7. forget, not remember      recall

**8.** one-sided, separate _____mutual_____

**9.** starting, beginning _____completion_____

# Word Riddles
Answer each riddle with a word from the box. Write the word on the line.

| | | | |
|---|---|---|---|
| cell | yearn | bureau | fraud |
| inconsiderate | greedily | boast | disassemble |

**1.** I am a noun.
I am a piece of furniture.
I am a synonym of *cabinet*.

I am _____bureau_____.

**2.** I am an adjective.
I describe a rude person.
I begin with a prefix.

I am _____inconsiderate_____.

**3.** I am a verb.
I mean "to break down or take apart."
I am an antonym of *build*.

I am _____disassemble_____.

**4.** I am a noun.
I am a part of every living thing.
I rhyme with *well*.

I am _____cell_____.

**5.** I am a verb.
I am a habit others get tired of hearing.
I am a synonym of *brag*.

I am _____boast_____.

**6.** I am a verb.
I mean "to want badly or long for."
I rhyme with *turn*.

I am _____yearn_____.

**7.** I am a noun.
I am a dishonest person or scheme.
I am a synonym of *cheating*.

I am _____fraud_____.

**8.** I am an adverb.
I can describe the way a person eats.
I am an antonym of *unselfishly*.

I am _____greedily_____.

# Posttest

## Choosing the Definitions

Fill in the bubble next to the item that best defines the word in bold in each sentence.

**Ch. 2  1.** The late nineteenth century was an era of great westward **migration.**
  a. direction  b. view  **c. movement**  d. retreat

**Ch. 8  2.** From the top of the mountain, we could **survey** the scene below.
  **a. inspect**  b. enjoy  c. paint  d. organize

**Ch. 6  3.** Fill out your application and give it to the program **administrator.**
  a. office  b. participant  **c. director**  d. helper

**Ch. 9  4.** The king's army was surprised by the sudden **revolt.**
  a. loud noise  b. trembling  **c. uprising**  d. illness

**Ch. 4  5.** After a delay at the beginning, we **progressed** rapidly.
  a. finished  **b. advanced**  c. stopped  d. delivered

**Ch. 2  6.** Austin used a toy to **distract** the baby from pulling on the lamp cord.
  **a. divert**  b. punish  c. annoy  d. teach

**Ch. 7  7.** Ethan didn't realize that his hurtful **comment** was heard at the next table.
  a. grip  **b. remark**  c. exercise  d. song

**Ch. 4  8.** Maybe reading the movie's review will **prompt** Victoria to come with us.
  a. demand  b. challenge  c. forbid  **d. encourage**

**Ch. 3  9.** Rachel is in charge of **circulation** for the school newspaper.
  **a. sending around**  b. editing  c. writing  d. folding

**Ch. 4  10.** Anna was delighted by the chance **encounter** with her old friend.
  a. call  **b. meeting**  c. gift  d. illness

**Ch. 4  11.** "We need to make some new rules about the **uncivilized** behavior in the lunchroom," Sydney declared.
  a. proper  b. odd  **c. wild**  d. annoying

**Ch. 8  12.** Destiny tried to **suppress** a yawn during the boring program.
  **a. smother**  b. let out  c. sleep  d. allow

**Ch. 1  13.** Our new car came with a one-year **guarantee.**
  a. plan  **b. promise**  c. trip  d. delay

**Ch. 2  14.** The captain depended on lighted buoys to help him pass through the **channel** at night.
  a. darkness  b. light mist  c. doorway  **d. deep water**

Ch. 5 **15.** Noah always felt **sentimental** when he thought of his old neighborhood.
(a.) angry    (b.) emotional    (c.) unhappy    (d.) abandoned

Ch. 6 **16.** Morgan said the new boy was handsome, but I thought he had a **sinister** grin.
(a.) threatening    (b.) ugly    (c.) childish    (d.) wide

Ch. 1 **17.** Jonathan hoped the dentist would not find any cavities during his **routine** checkup.
(a.) rare    (b.) boring    (c.) regular    (d.) canceled

Ch. 6 **18.** The **ravine** in our backyard makes a good hiding place.
(a.) valley    (b.) playhouse    (c.) oak    (d.) hill

Ch. 5 **19.** Every so often, I like to find a quiet spot and **contemplate** life.
(a.) forget about    (b.) reflect on    (c.) remember    (d.) pursue

Ch. 5 **20.** For Christian, an **ideal** vacation is a week on the ski slopes.
(a.) ruined    (b.) relaxing    (c.) perfect    (d.) free

Ch. 4 **21.** Jennifer won first prize for her **exceptional** painting.
(a.) colorful    (b.) modern    (c.) strange    (d.) outstanding

Ch. 4 **22.** On our field trip to the museum, we saw many **classic** works of art.
(a.) modern    (b.) colorful    (c.) excellent    (d.) interesting

Ch. 1 **23.** It is impossible to ride a bicycle on this rocky **terrain**.
(a.) land    (b.) roadway    (c.) journey    (d.) shore

Ch. 8 **24.** Some **legends** were created to explain things people did not understand.
(a.) lectures    (b.) old stories    (c.) formulas    (d.) paintings

Ch. 2 **25.** Only groups with guides were allowed to use the **perilous** hiking trail.
(a.) risky    (b.) scenic    (c.) expensive    (d.) natural

Ch. 8 **26.** Jasmine moved slowly and **deliberately** toward the roaring dragon.
(a.) swiftly    (b.) timidly    (c.) purposefully    (d.) carelessly

Ch. 9 **27.** Haley turned down the job because she felt that the **compensation** was not adequate.
(a.) workplace    (b.) title    (c.) hours    (d.) pay

Ch. 3 **28.** Rebecca listened carefully to the astrologer's **prediction**.
(a.) song    (b.) foretelling    (c.) tale    (d.) memory

Ch. 2 **29.** Dylan was a good nurse because he treated his patients with **compassion**.
(a.) rudeness    (b.) skill    (c.) kindness    (d.) coolness

Ch. 3 **30.** Stephanie had a **novel** idea for her science project.
(a.) unusual    (b.) dangerous    (c.) boring    (d.) difficult

## Word Relations

Synonyms are words that have the same or nearly the same meanings. Antonyms are words that have opposite or nearly opposite meanings.

In the blank before each pair of words, write *S* if the words are synonyms, *A* if they are antonyms, or *N* if they are not related.

| | | | | | | |
|---|---|---|---|---|---|---|
| 1. | N | protein | pulse | 16. | S | mercy | compassion |
| 2. | N | accumulate | molecule | 17. | N | parasite | vertebra |
| 3. | A | inconsiderate | respectful | 18. | A | clarify | complicate |
| 4. | S | irritate | annoy | 19. | S | triumphant | victorious |
| 5. | N | traitor | treaty | 20. | N | coarse | numb |
| 6. | S | incidental | unexpected | 21. | S | sinister | forbidding |
| 7. | N | inherent | victorious | 22. | A | imperfect | ideal |
| 8. | A | abolish | preserve | 23. | N | circumference | cell |
| 9. | N | fraud | common | 24. | N | bureau | debris |
| 10. | S | scheme | tactic | 25. | S | common | mutual |
| 11. | S | clarify | illustrate | 26. | S | imperfect | impure |
| 12. | N | orbit | injection | 27. | N | legislator | infantry |
| 13. | N | issue | frame | 28. | A | magnify | reduce |
| 14. | A | compliment | criticize | 29. | N | parliament | theory |
| 15. | N | caravan | abandon | 30. | S | ambition | intention |

## Using Context Clues

Use the word in bold and the sentence context to underline the phrase that best completes each sentence.

Ch. 9   1.   A **wedge** is useful as a
      (a.) ladder.
      (b.) saw.
      (c.) doorstop.
      (d.) chair.

Ch. 6   2.   If you go to a **convention**, you will probably
      (a.) spend a lot of time alone.
      (b.) meet many new people.
      (c.) invent something useful.
      (d.) see classic words of art.

Ch. 3   **3.**   If you like to **harmonize**, you like to

- **a.** carry a tune.
- **b.** make up after a quarrel.
- **c.** tell jokes.
- **d.** bake fancy desserts.

Ch. 9   **4.**   If someone speaks of her distant **destination**, she may be referring to

- **a.** a relative.
- **b.** her dentist.
- **c.** her favorite star.
- **d.** her travel plans.

Ch. 7   **5.**   The man accused of murder was **framed**; he was

- **a.** made to look guilty.
- **b.** photographed.
- **c.** famous.
- **d.** frightened.

Ch. 3   **6.**   If you sound **hoarse**, you might have a

- **a.** toothache.
- **b.** sore throat.
- **c.** pony.
- **d.** fear of speaking in public.

Ch. 1   **7.**   Maria rented a **furnished** apartment because she didn't have any

- **a.** food.
- **b.** time.
- **c.** carpeting.
- **d.** furniture.

Ch. 1   **8.**   The nineteenth **century** lasted

- **a.** one hundred years.
- **b.** nineteen years.
- **c.** nineteen months.
- **d.** one hundred days.

Ch. 5   **9.**   If you have a **contraction** in your muscle, your muscle probably feels

- **a.** relaxed.
- **b.** itchy.
- **c.** cramped.
- **d.** warm.

Ch. 9   **10.**   If you can **relate** apples to oranges, you can

- **a.** show how they are different.
- **b.** set them next to each other.
- **c.** do a magic trick.
- **d.** show how they are the same.

Ch. 8   **11.**   When the queen's **reign** ended, she

- **a.** put away her umbrella.
- **b.** shouted "Bravo!"
- **c.** lost her power.
- **d.** lost her memory.

Ch. 6   **12.**   A person whose hobby is **vaulting** probably

- **a.** likes to fly through the air.
- **b.** likes to go underground.
- **c.** is afraid of heights.
- **d.** enjoys the water.

**Ch. 6 13.** Todd felt a bit **squeamish** as he

    (a.) listened to the soft music.

    (b.) drifted off to sleep.

    (c.) chewed his favorite gum.

    (d.) watched the horror movie.

**Ch. 9 14.** Upon her **completion** of the bike race, Sophia felt

    (a.) ashamed that she dropped out.

    (b.) proud that she finished.

    (c.) worried about her flat tire.

    (d.) afraid she'd never make it.

**Ch. 6 15.** If you buy an **imperfect** pair of shoes, they may

    (a.) not fit.

    (b.) last a long time.

    (c.) feel great.

    (d.) look great.

**Ch. 2 16.** **Testimony** is often given

    (a.) at a party.

    (b.) in outer space.

    (c.) in a court of law.

    (d.) in a hospital.

**Ch. 1 17.** **Pneumonia** is a disease that affects

    (a.) farm animals.

    (b.) the lungs.

    (c.) the spine.

    (d.) houseplants.

**Ch. 3 18.** If you could ride in a **satellite**, you would be

    (a.) under the ground.

    (b.) in the water.

    (c.) in outer space.

    (d.) on a railroad track.

**Ch. 7 19.** People who **boast**

    (a.) love snowy weather.

    (b.) brag about things they own.

    (c.) are modest about their talents.

    (d.) are usually very good cooks.

**Ch. 5 20.** You may get a **vaccine**

    (a.) in a doctor's office.

    (b.) on a tropical island.

    (c.) in an appliance store.

    (d.) in an apartment building.

**Ch. 2 21.** To care for a **guppy**, you must

    (a.) take it for walks.

    (b.) teach it to fetch.

    (c.) brush it every day.

    (d.) change its water.

**Ch. 6 22.** A coat of **shellac**

    (a.) can keep you warm.

    (b.) is made of fur.

    (c.) can be put on a table.

    (d.) is usually called a jacket.

**Ch. 8 23.** A person wearing a **manacle** probably

 (a.) is wealthy.  (c.) has poor vision.

 **(b.)** is a prisoner.  (d.) is a child.

**Ch. 9 24.** Someone who eats **greedily**

 **(a.)** is eating everything in sight.  (c.) only eats dessert.

 (b.) is using good manners.  (d.) is a very picky eater.

**Ch. 5 25.** If you are **awkward,**

 (a.) you would make a good dancer.  (c.) you would make a good athlete.

 (b.) you are very intelligent.  **(d.)** you often bump into things.

**Ch. 4 26.** An **annual** event

 (a.) takes place once a month.  **(c.)** takes place every year.

 (b.) takes place in the city.  (d.) takes place in a park.

**Ch. 2 27.** If you make an **appeal,** you

 (a.) cook a fruit pie.  (c.) will use a sewing machine.

 **(b.)** ask for help.  (d.) donate some money.

**Ch. 6 28.** Farmers use an **irrigation** system to

 (a.) plow their fields.  (c.) feed their animals.

 (b.) harvest their crops.  **(d.)** water their crops.

**Ch. 7 29.** An **aggressive** dog

 **(a.)** may attack as you walk by.  (c.) will run if you come near it.

 (b.) has won a prize at a dog show.  (d.) never barks at strangers.

**Ch. 4 30.** A person who is a **nuisance**

 (a.) is fun to be around.  **(c.)** is an annoying pest.

 (b.) has a lot of money.  (d.) has just moved next door.

## Test-Taking Tips

Taking a standardized test can be difficult. Here are a few things you can do to make the experience easier.

Get a good night's sleep the night before the test. You want to be alert and rested in the morning.

Eat a healthful breakfast. Your brain needs good food to work properly.

Wear layers of clothing. You can take off or put on a layer if you get too warm or too cold.

Bring two sharp number 2 pencils with erasers.

When you get the test, read the directions carefully. Be sure you understand what you are supposed to do. If you have any questions, ask your teacher before you start marking your answers.

If you feel nervous, close your eyes and take a deep breath as you silently count to three. Then slowly breathe out. Do this several times until your mind is calm.

Manage your time. Check to see how many questions there are. Try to answer half the questions before half the time is up.

Answer the easy questions first. If you don't know the answer to a question, skip it and come back to it later if you have time.

Try to answer all the questions. Some will seem very hard, but don't worry about it. Nobody is expected to get every answer right. Make the best guess you can.

If you make a mistake, erase it completely. Then write the correct answer or fill in the correct circle.

When you have finished, go back over the test. Work on any questions you skipped. Check your answers.

## Question Types

Many tests contain the same kinds of questions. Here are a few of the question types that you may encounter.

## Meaning from Context

This kind of question asks you to figure out the meaning of a word from the words or sentences around it.

> The smoke from the smoldering garbage made her eyes water.

Which word in the sentence helps you understand the meaning of *smoldering*?

| | |
|---|---|
| smoke | garbage |
| eyes | water |

Read the sentence carefully. You know that smoke comes from something that is burning. *Smoldering* must mean "burning." *Smoke* is the correct answer.

## Synonyms and Antonyms

Some questions ask you to identify the synonym of a word. Synonyms are words that have the same or nearly the same meaning. Some questions ask you to identify the antonym of a word. Antonyms are words that have the opposite or nearly the opposite meaning.

The workers buffed the statue until it shone like a mirror.

Which word is a synonym for *buffed*?

polished            covered

tarnished          dismantled

Read the answers carefully. Which word means "to make something shine"? The answer is *polish*.

When she feels morose, she watches funny cartoons to change her mood.

Which word is an antonym of *morose*?

dismal              agreeable

happy              confident

Think about the sentence. If something funny will change her mood, she must be sad. The answer is *happy*, the antonym of *sad*.

## Analogies

This kind of question asks you to find relationships between pairs of words. Analogies usually use *is to* and *as*.

**green** is to **grass** as _____ is to **sky**

Green is the color of grass. So the answer must be **blue**, the color of the sky.

## Roots

A root is a building block for words. Many roots come from ancient languages such as Greek or Latin. Knowing the meaning of a root can often help you figure out the meaning of a word. Note that sometimes the spelling of the root changes.

| Root | Language | Meaning | Example |
|------|----------|---------|---------|
| audi | Latin | to hear | audience audible auditorium |
| bibl | Greek | book | bibliography Bible bibliophile |
| cred | Latin | to believe | credence creed incredible |
| dict | Greek | to speak | predict dictionary dictation |
| finis | Latin | end, limit | finish finally infinite |
| graph | Greek | to write or draw | autograph biography paragraph |
| scribe | Latin | to write | describe subscribe prescribe |

## Prefixes

A prefix is a word part added to the beginning of a base word. A prefix changes the meaning of the base word.

| Prefix | Meaning | Base Word | Example |
|--------|---------|-----------|---------|
| dis- | not, opposite of | like | dislike |
| mid- | in the middle of | air | midair |
| mis- | badly, wrongly | behave | misbehave |
| pre- | before, earlier | cook | precook |
| re- | again | paint | repaint |
| sub- | under | freezing | subfreezing |
| tele- | far away | photo | telephoto |
| un- | not | happy | unhappy |
| under- | below, less than | foot | underfoot |

# Suffixes

## Suffixes

A suffix is a word part added to the end of a base word. A suffix changes the meaning of the base word. Sometimes the base word changes spelling when a suffix is added.

| Suffix | Meaning | Base Word | Example |
|---|---|---|---|
| -able | able to be, full of | agree | agreeable |
| -al | relating to | music | musical |
| -ate | to make | active | activate |
| -en | to become, to make | light | lighten |
| -er | person who | teach | teacher |
| | | run | runner |
| -ful | full of | cheer | cheerful |
| | | beauty | beautiful |
| -fy | to make | simple | simplify |
| -ic | like a, relating to | artist | artistic |
| | | athlete | athletic |
| -ish | like a, resembling | child | childish |
| -ize | to cause to be | legal | legalize |
| | | apology | apologize |
| -less | without | hope | hopeless |
| | | penny | penniless |
| -ly, -ally | in a (certain) way | sad | sadly |
| | | magic | magically |
| -ship | a state of being | friend | friendship |
| -ward | in the direction of | east | eastward |
| -y | like, full of | thirst | thirsty |
| | | fog | foggy |

## My Vocabulary in Action Dictionary

**Categories:** *Individual, Visual Learners*

Create your own dictionary of vocabulary words. Take 14 sheets of white paper and one sheet of construction paper and fold them in half. Place the white paper inside the folded construction paper to create a book. Staple the book together on the fold. Label each page of your book with one letter of the alphabet.

At the end of each vocabulary chapter, enter the new words into your dictionary. Include the word, the definition, the part of speech, and a sentence. Each definition should be written in your own words. This will be a good tool to use throughout the year.

## Vocabulary Challenge

**Category:** *Small Group*

Prepare for the game by choosing 15 vocabulary words from the current chapter. Write each word on a separate index card. On the back of the card, write the definition of the word. Place the cards on the floor, with the definition-side down, in three rows of five cards.

Three or four players sit facing the cards. The first player points to a word and gives its definition. If the player gives the correct definition, he or she gets to keep the card. If the player gives the wrong definition, he or she returns the card to the floor.

Players take turns until all the cards are gone. The player with the most cards wins the game.

## Vocabulary Quilt

**Categories:** *Individual or Small Group, Visual Learners*

Find one or two friends to help create a "vocabulary quilt," or create a quilt of your own. Write each vocabulary word from the current chapter in big letters across the top of a separate sheet of construction paper. Illustrate each word, using markers or colored pencils. As you finish, place the pictures in a quilt-like arrangement on a bulletin board. Leave the pictures posted in the room and allow the other students to "visually" learn their vocabulary words.

## Toss the Ball

**Categories:** *Small Group, Kinesthetic Learners*

Find four friends and sit in a circle on the floor. Your group will need a ball and a list of the current chapter's vocabulary words. The first person with the ball says a vocabulary word aloud, then quickly tosses the ball to another person in the group. That person must correctly define the word. If successful, that person says another vocabulary word and tosses the ball to another player. If the word is not defined correctly, the player must leave the circle. The game continues until there is only one player remaining.

© Loyola Press.

For an additional challenge, say a synonym or an antonym for the word instead of a definition.

## Synonym Partners

### Category: *Large Group*

Write the current chapter's vocabulary words on index cards. Then write a synonym for each word on additional cards. Divide the class into two groups and give the words to one group and the synonyms to the other group.

The object of the game is for each student to find the appropriate synonym partner without speaking or using body language. The partners sit on the floor once they find each other. After all partners are found, each pair tells the class the vocabulary word, its synonym, and the definition.

This game may also be played using an antonym of the vocabulary word instead of a synonym. For a greater challenge, play the game using both a synonym and an antonym without using the vocabulary word.

## Catch That Plate

### Categories: *Small Group, Kinesthetic Learners*

Write the vocabulary words from the current chapter on slips of paper and place them in a hat. Ask the players to sit in a circle on the floor. Place the hat and a plastic plate in the center. The first player goes to the center of the circle, takes a slip of paper, reads the word, names another player, and spins the plate. The player whose name was called must quickly give a definition for the vocabulary word and then "catch the plate" before it comes to a stop. If successful, that player becomes the new plate spinner. If that player fails to catch the plate in time, the same plate spinner remains.

## Vocabulary Egg Shake

### Category: *Partners, Kinesthetic Learners*

Find a partner and write the current chapter's vocabulary words on slips of paper. Glue these slips to the inside of each cup section of an egg carton. Place a penny in the egg carton and close the carton. The first partner shakes the carton and then lifts the lid. The second partner must state the correct definition of the vocabulary word on which the penny landed. If successful, he or she must shake the carton. For a variation to this game, state the synonym or antonym for the vocabulary word instead of the definition.

This activity can be used for each new vocabulary chapter by replacing the vocabulary words with new words.

## Vocabulary Search

**Categories:** *Small Group,*
*Kinesthetic Learners,*
*ELL*

Form a group of five students. Create alphabet cards from cardboard. Cut out 75 small squares and write one letter of the alphabet on each square. Make two alphabets plus several additional squares for each vowel.

Place the alphabet squares in two piles —with the same letters in each pile—in the middle of the playing area. Designate one person to be the announcer. The remaining four players break into teams of two. The game begins when the announcer says a definition, a synonym, or an antonym of one of the current chapter's vocabulary words. Then each team uses the alphabet cards to try to spell the word to which the announcer is referring. The first team to correctly spell the word receives one point. The team with the most points at the end of the game wins.

## Vocabulary Baseball

**Category:** *Small Group*

Prepare for the game by drawing a baseball diamond on a sheet of paper. Be sure to include three bases and home plate. Write on index cards all of the current chapter's vocabulary words, along with their definitions. Find three friends and divide into two teams. Determine how many innings there will be in the game.

The first team at bat sends its player to home plate. The first player on the other team "pitches" a word to the batter by reading a word. If the batter correctly states the definition, he or she moves to first base. The player continues to move from base to base until he or she crosses home plate or misses the definition. When a player misses, the team gets an out. After three outs, the other team is at bat.

When a player crosses home plate, the team gets one point and the next player bats. The team with the most points at the end of the last inning wins the game.

# Vocabulary Fables

**Categories:** *Individual,*
*Visual Learners*

Reread a popular fairy tale, such as "Cinderella" or "The Three Little Pigs." After you have finished reading the story, write your own version, using at least 10 vocabulary words from the current chapter. Make your new story into a book with illustrated pages and a construction-paper cover. Share your story with your classmates or with another class.

# Comic-Strip Vocabulary

**Categories:** *Individual,*
*Visual Learners*

Prepare for the game by bringing to class some examples of comic strips from newspapers or magazines. Look over the examples for ideas to create your own comic strip. You can either make up new comic-strip characters or use existing characters. Fold a sheet of paper into six equal parts to create six frames. Use at least four of the current chapter's vocabulary words in your story. You should fill each frame with words and pictures. You might display your comic strip or share it with classmates.

# Vocabulary Tic-Tac-Toe

**Category:** *Partners*

Prepare for the game by writing the current chapter's vocabulary words on index cards. Write the definition of the word on the back of the card. You will also need to create five *X* and five *O* cards. Place the vocabulary cards, definition-side down, in a stack. Draw a large tic-tac-toe board on a sheet of paper. Cover each square with a vocabulary card, definition-side down.

Work with a partner. The first player chooses a word and says the definition. If the player is correct, he or she removes the card and replaces it with an *X*. If the player is incorrect, the card goes to the bottom of the vocabulary stack and is replaced with a new card. Then the second player chooses a word and tries to define it. The game continues until a player has successfully made a "tic-tac-toe." This game can be played many times by shuffling the vocabulary cards between rounds.

# Word Search Puzzles

**Categories:** *Partners,*
*Auditory Learners*

Prepare for the game by bringing to class examples of word search puzzles from newspapers, magazines, or books. You will need one sheet of graph paper and a pencil. Use the examples to guide you in creating a word search puzzle that includes some of the vocabulary words from the current chapter. On another sheet of paper, write the definitions of the words you included.

When you have finished your word search puzzle, exchange it with a friend. Take turns reading aloud your definition clues. Your partner must guess the correct vocabulary word and find it in your word search puzzle. Return the word search puzzle to the appropriate owner to check for accuracy.

# Tell Me a Story

**Category:** *Small Group*

Find three partners. You will need two sheets of paper and a pen or pencil. Write all the vocabulary words from the current chapter on one sheet of notebook paper.

One person in the group begins creating a story by writing a sentence or two, using one of the vocabulary words. That person then passes the paper to the next group member. Each player is allowed to use only one vocabulary word each turn. The object of the game is to use all the vocabulary words correctly to form a complete story. The story must make sense, and it must have a beginning, a middle, and an end. Ask someone to check your story for accuracy.

# Vocabulary Role-Play

**Categories:** *Small Group,*
*Kinesthetic Learners,*
*ELL*

Find two partners. Pick 15 vocabulary words from the current chapter. Write each word on a separate small slip of paper. Fold the slips of paper in half and place them in a hat.

Each person selects a word from the hat. When it's your turn, take two minutes to develop a short skit about your word to perform for your partners. In the skit, you must act out your vocabulary word without saying the word. The first person to guess the word correctly draws the next word.

# Jeopardy

**Categories:** *Small Group,*
*Auditory Learners*

Work with three partners. One player starts by giving the definition of a current chapter's vocabulary word. The other three players try to guess the word as quickly as possible. (They do not have to wait for the entire definition.) The first one to guess the word correctly gets to give the next definition. Keep track of who correctly guesses the most words.

# Words in Context

**Categories:** *Partners,*
*Technology,*
*ELL*

Work with a partner at a computer. One person enters a vocabulary word from the current chapter. Then the second person enters a sentence using that word correctly. Take turns entering words and sentences. See how many you can complete in 10 minutes. (If you do not have access to a computer, you can write the words and sentences on a sheet of paper.)

# Concentration

**Categories:** *Partners,*
*Visual Learners,*
*ELL*

Write eight of the current chapter's vocabulary words on separate index cards. Write the definitions of the words on eight more index cards. Shuffle the cards and place them facedown in a square with four rows of four cards.

Work with a partner. One person turns over two cards. If the definition matches the word, that player keeps the cards. If the definition does not match the word, the player puts the cards facedown in the same places they were before. The other player then turns over two cards. Continue until all the cards have been taken. The partner with the most pairs of cards wins the game.

## A Word a Day

**Category:** *Large Group*

Each morning, write one of the current chapter's vocabulary words on the board. Encourage the students to use that word throughout the day. Keep track of how many times the word is used.

## Hangman

**Category:** *Large Group*

On the board, draw a short line for each letter in a word. Read the definition of the word and have the students guess it by naming its letters. As each letter is called out, write it on the correct line.

## Listen to This

**Categories:** *Individual, Auditory Learners, ELL, Technology*

Some students, such as those who are not strong readers, will benefit from repeated listening. Record each vocabulary word followed by a slight pause and then its definition. Let individuals listen to the complete recording several times. Then have them listen to each word, stop the recorder, and define the word themselves. They can then listen to the definition to make sure they were correct.

## Same or Opposite?

**Categories:** *Partner or Small Group, ELL*

This activity will provide reteaching and reinforcement for students who need it. Prepare index cards by writing each vocabulary word on one side and a synonym or an antonym on the other side. Have partners or a small group take turns drawing the cards, reading the two words, and telling whether they are synonyms or antonyms.

## Sentence Challenge

**Category:** *Individual or Small Group*

For reteaching and reinforcement, write a group of sentences, each using one of the vocabulary words. However, put the letters of the vocabulary word in alphabetical order instead of spelling it correctly. Challenge individuals or partners to figure out the word and spell it.

## Find the Words

**Category:** *Large Group*

Encourage students to look for the current chapter's vocabulary words throughout a week. Remind them to look not only in books, magazines, and newspapers, but also on signs, in directions, and in ads. Tell students to listen for the words on the radio or TV. Have the students write down each word and where they saw or heard it. At the end of the week, count up how many times each word was found.

# Be a Star

**Categories:** *Small Group,*
*Technology*

Have students work together in small groups to write skits containing as many of the current chapter's vocabulary words as possible. Make a video of each group performing its skit for the whole class.

Here is a list of all the words defined in this book. The number following each word indicates the page on which the word is defined. The Challenge Words are listed in *italics*. The Word Study Words are listed in **bold**.

abandon, 7
abolish, 27
absolute, 75
abundant, 75
abuse, 17
accommodate, 19
accumulate, 27
acquaint, 41
acquire, 43
acre, 51
**actor**, 5
adequate, 28
adjust, 61
*administer*, 13
administrator, 62
admirable, 75
aggressive, 76
alarm, 85
ambition, 7
annoy, 8
annual, 43
*antagonize*, 57
*antiquated*, 33
appeal, 17
ascent, 15
ascribe, 83
assent, 15
astonish, 28
atmosphere, 41
authorship, 73
awkward, 53

**bacteria**, 39
*baffle*, 57
boast, 76
**brothers-in-law**, 39
*brusque*, 91
buff, 85
bureau, 87

*camouflage*, 13
**capital**, 15
**capitol**, 15
caravan, 95
cell, 96

*centennial*, 13
century, 7
**championship**, 73
channel, 17
charge, 19
circulation, 27
circumference, 28
clarify, 41
classic, 43
classify, 51
clot, 53
coarse, 61
combat, 8
*combustible*, 13
comment, 76
common, 85
commotion, 87
compassion, 19
compensation, 96
competition, 95
*compile*, 33
completion, 96
complicate, 8
compliment, 17
compromise, 62
conclude, 27
*confederate*, 57
*confirm*, 101
*conflict*, 101
conjunction, 28
conscience, 41
consist, 43
contemplate, 51
contraction, 53
convention, 61
*corrode*, 57
**counselor**, 5
course, 62
**crises**, 39
criticize, 75
cultivate, 76

debris, 7
*defer*, 101
*deficient*, 33

*deflect*, 67
*deliberately*, 87
*dependent*, 33
**describe**, 83
destination, 95
*deteriorate*, 67
*devastate*, 67
*devout*, 47
*dexterity*, 91
*diffuse*, 67
disassemble, 96
*dismal*, 13
*dissension*, 67
distract, 17
*dwindle*, 47

earnest, 19
encounter, 41
*endurance*, 23
*envious*, 23
exceptional, 43
*exempt*, 48
*expenditure*, 81
explore, 51
**explorer**, 5
export, 53

*fastidious*, 81
forbidding, 61
frame, 75
fraud, 77
**friendship**, 73
frontier, 85
furnish, 8
*furrow*, 23

*gaudy*, 81
genuine, 87
greedily, 96
guarantee, 7
guppy, 17

haggard, 62
**hangar**, 15
**hanger**, 15
harmonize, 27

hoarse, 28
homogenize, 41
*humility*, 81

ideal, 51
illustrate, 53
*impenetrable*, 48
imperfect, 61
impure, 75
*incessant*, 92
incident, 77
incidental, 85
inconsiderate, 87
indigo, 95
industry, 97
ineffective, 7
inexpensive, 8
infantry, 17
infection, 19
inflammable, 27
influence, 29
inherent, 19
injection, 43
insane, 51
**inscribe**, 83
intention, 53
**inventor**, 5
irrigation, 61
irritate, 63
issue, 75

kerosene, 77
**kinship**, 73

legend, 85
legislator, 61

magnificent, 87
magnify, 95
manacle, 85
**manager**, 5
mentality, 7
mercy, 9
**midair**, 49
**midnight**, 49
**midsize**, 49

© Loyola Press.

midterm, 49
midwinter, 49
midyear, 49
migration, 17
*mingle,* 24
*modesty,* 24
molecule, 19
mutual, 95

nimble, 41
nourish, 27
novel, 29
nuisance, 43
numb, 51

oblige, 61
observe, 63
orbit, 85
orient, 53
**oxen,** 39

*paltry,* 81
parasite, 87
parliament, 95
*peerless,* 92
perilous, 19
pneumonia, 7
pod, 9

*pompous,* 92
*precipitate,* 101
prediction, 27
**prescribe,** 83
preserve, 29
progress, 41
prompt, 43
**proscribe,** 83
protein, 51
pulse, 53

ravine, 63
recall, 75
reclaim, 77
*recur,* 48
reduce, 85
reign, 87
relate, 95
remedy, 97
respectful, 7
revolt, 97
routine, 9

salvation, 17
sanity, 19
satellite, 27
*saturate,* 33
scandal, 29

scheme, 42
**scholarship,** 73
security, 43
seep, 53
sentimental, 52
shellac, 61
sinister, 63
solace, 9
**sportsmanship,** 73
squeamish, 61
*steep,* 101
sterilize, 63
stern, 75
strive, 77
**subfreezing,** 93
**submarine,** 93
**submerge,** 93
**subscribe,** 83
**subsoil,** 93
**substandard,** 93
**subway,** 93
suppress, 87
survey, 87
survival, 95

tactics, 97
**teeth,** 39
**telecommunicate,** 25

**telephone,** 25
**telephoto,** 25
**telescope,** 25
**television,** 25
temptation, 7
terrain, 9
testimony, 18
theory, 19
traitor, 27
treaty, 29
triumphant, 42

uncivilized, 43
unexpected, 52

vaccine, 53
*vain,* 58
vault, 63
vertebra, 75
victorious, 77
vivid, 85

wedge, 95
**women,** 39
**writer,** 5

yearn, 97

*Index of Words    Level E*